the great *lobster* and crab cookbook

THE GREAT LOBSTER AND CRAB COOKBOOK

Published by:
R&R Publications Marketing Pty. Ltd
ACN 083 612 579
PO Box 254, Carlton North, Victoria 3054 Australia
Phone (61 3) 9381 2199 Fax (61 3) 9381 2689
E-mail: richardc@bigpond.net.au
Australia-wide toll free: 1800 063 296

The Great Lobster and Crab Cookbook

Publisher: Richard Carroll
Production Manager: Anthony Carroll
Designer: Vincent Wee
Creative Director: Paul Sims
Computer Graphics: Lucy Adams
Food Photography: Gary Smith
Food Stylist: Janet Lodge
Food for Photography: Louise Hockham and Katrina Cleary
Recipe Development: Ellen Argyriou, Janet Lodge and Lyn Carroll, Tamara Milstein (23)
Proof Reader: Fiona Brodribb

The publishers would like to thank the management and staff of the Prince Edward Island Department of Fisheries and Aquaculture, especially Mr. Parnell Trainor, for their assistance in providing information and recipes pertaining to the Northern Lobster.

The National Library of Australia
Cataloguing-in-Publication Data
The Great Lobster and Crab Cookbook
Includes Index
ISBN 1 74022 152 4
EAN 9 781740 221 528

First Edition Printed August 2002
Computer Typeset in Verdana, Trojan and Charcoal

Printed in Singapore

contents

INTRODUCTION

Sink your teeth into our succulent crab and lobster dishes. We have gathered together recipes that elicit the best flavours from these fabulous foods from the sea. From soups that flood your house with blissful aromas to main meals that are bursting with colour in a celebration of the world's most treasured cuisine, you are bound to enjoy every mouthful.

We have provided signposts on your journey, with expert advice on how to prepare, cook, clean and store crab and lobster to attain the most tender, mouth-watering tastes. A few secrets revealed will mean you can determine whether your seafood is fresh, and other tips will ensure that your results match those found in even the finest, silver-service restaurants. So prepare yourself to be lavished in luxury, because words cannot describe what you are about to experience.

CRAB PREPARATION

To Store

Wrap the crab in plastic wrap or foil or store in an airtight container in the refrigerator for up to 3 days or you can freeze up to 3 months providing your freezer operates at -18°C/0°F.

To Prepare a Crab

For green or cooked crabs, insert the point of a knife at 'seam' area where the top shell meets the base (the opposite side of the eyes). Using a lever action lift off the shell. Wash the inside thoroughly and remove the meat if necessary. Break off the claws and snap with a shellfish cracker to remove the meat, or segment into quarters.

To Cook a Crab

The most humane method to cook live crabs is to place the crab into the freezer for several hours. This method does not freeze the meat but has an anaesthetising effect on the crab. (Never plunge into boiling water as this toughens the meat and the claws can fall off. It is also generally thought to be more painful for the crab). Alternatively, to kill the crab instantly, stab it just behind the eyes with the point of a sharp knife (step 1). Place the crab into cold water, cover the pan and bring to boil. Simmer 5–20 minutes (depending upon size).

The crab is cooked when it turns a bright orange colour. A great way to eat crab is cold with lemon and freshly ground black pepper. The meat is sweet and succulent and requires little else. It goes well with lemon, lime, parsley, coriander (cilantro) and thyme and is ideal served with fruits and salad vegetables.

To Clean Crab

Place the crab on its back, and gently fold back the tail flap or apron. Twist and pull the apron off. You will find that the intestinal vein is attached and will pull out along the apron. Discard (step 2).

Hold the crab with one hand where the apron was removed. Use the other hand to pry up, tear-off and discard the top shell.

Remove the gills, take out the greyish bag and pull out mandibles from the front of the crab (step 3).

Hold the body where the legs were attached and apply pressure so that the crab splits in half along the centre of the body. Fold back the halves and twist apart (step 4).

Twist off the claws and legs where they join the body. Crack with a hammer or nutcracker to make the meat easy to remove.

Step 1

Step 2

Step 3

Step 4

LOBSTER PREPARATION

How to Buy lobster

Lobsters may be purchased live in the shell, or freshly cooked in the shell. When purchased live, lobster should show some movement and the tail should spring back when straightened out. Lobsters that show no movement when handled and have a tail that hangs down straight, are dead and should be discarded.

When handling live lobster, be careful of the claws (if they have any) as they can give you a severe pinch. To protect the handler and to prevent the lobster from harming each other in captivity, the claws are usually immobilised by placing an elastic band around them.

When buying cooked lobster, check that they are a bright 'red-orange' colour and have a fresh aroma. The tail section should spring back into a curled position after being straightened out.

How to Store

Live lobster should never be placed in fresh water or on ice. Under ideal cool, damp storage conditions, lobster can live out of water for up to 36 hours. They can be stored in your refrigerator for several hours by placing them in a large container covered with damp newspaper or seaweed. Cooked lobster in the shell can be stored in the refrigerator for up to 2 days if placed in a tightly covered container. Shucked lobster meat can be refrigerated for 2–3 days.

Live lobsters should never be frozen but cooked lobster freezes well. For best results, the cooked meat should be removed from the shell and placed in plastic containers or freezer bags. Prepare a brine solution of 55g/2oz salt to each litre of fresh water. Pour this over the lobster so that all the meat is covered and a 1cm/1/2in headspace remains.

Whole cooked lobster can be frozen in individual heavy plastic bags. Place the lobster in the bag, being careful that the sharp shell does not puncture the bag, cover with a brine solution, then cover tightly and freeze.

To thaw lobster, place in the refrigerator and allow 18 hours for defrosting. To speed up defrosting time, place the package under cold running water until thawed.

How to Prepare

To cook live lobsters, the most humane way is to place the lobster in the freezer then simmer it as you would a crab. Lobster should be cooked either in clean sea water or salted fresh water. Lobster will cook in 12–20 minutes, depending on the size of the lobster. Once cooked, the lobster should be drained immediately. It can now be served hot or chilled quickly by dipping in cold water.

Cleaning Lobster

Hold the lobster right-side-up on a firm surface. Pierce the shell at the centre of the body, behind the head (step 1).

Cut the lobster in half lengthwise and remove and discard the sac near the head, and the intestinal vein in the tail. Remove any roe from the body and reserve for flavouring sauces (step 2).

Clean the lobster by rinsing under cold, running water (step 3).

Step 1

Step 2

Step 3

NUTRITIONAL INFORMATION

	Spanner Crab	Lobster
Protein	19.1	19.4
Fat	0.9	0.8
Kilojoules (Calories) per 100g	360	360
Saturated Fat (g) per 100g	0.3	0.2
Monounsaturated fat (g) per 100g	0.2	0.2
Total polyunsaturated fat (g) per 100g	0.4	0.4
Omega 3s (mg) per 100g edible portion	366	234
Cholesterol (mg) per edible portion	68	98

SOUPS & SALADS

Prawn and Crab Soup

INGREDIENTS

6 tomatoes, chopped

2 onions, chopped

1 tablespoon vegetable oil

4 cloves garlic, crushed

1 tablespoon oregano leaves

2 fresh coriander (cilantro) plants

1 fish head, such as snapper, perch,
cod or haddock

10 cups water

2 uncooked crabs, cleaned and
cut into serving pieces

12 medium uncooked prawns (shrimp)
shelled and deveined

200g/7oz fish fillet, cut into chunks

METHOD

1. Place the tomatoes and onions in a food processor or blender and process to make a purée.

2. Heat the oil in a saucepan over medium heat, add the garlic and cook, stirring, for 1 minute or until golden. Stir in the tomato mixture, then add oregano leaves and coriander (cilantro) plants. Bring to simmering point and simmer for 15 minutes. Add the fish head and water and simmer 20 for minutes. Strain stock and discard solids. Return the stock to a clean saucepan.

3. Add the crabs and prawns (shrimp) to the stock, bring to simmer and simmer for 3 minutes. Add the fish and simmer for 1–2 minutes or until all the seafood is cooked.

Serves 6

Lobster Salad with Red Devil Dressing

INGREDIENTS

1 bulb garlic

1/3 cup olive oil

salt

1/2 large onion

2 red capsicums (bell peppers)

1 large portabella mushroom,
lightly oiled

juice of 1/2 lemon

1 tablespoon dried fennel

1 tablespoon tomato sauce (ketchup)

1 tablespoon apple cider vinegar

ground black pepper

750g/26oz cooked lobster tails,
shredded and chilled

4 cups mixed salad greens

METHOD

1. Preheat the oven. Position the rack in the centre of the oven. Lightly oil a baking tray.

2. Cut off the top of the garlic and place on a square of aluminum foil. Drizzle with 1 teaspoon of olive oil, and sprinkle with a pinch of salt. Wrap in foil, and place on the baking tray. Prepare onion in the same manner.

3. Place baking tray in the centre of the oven and bake the garlic and onion for 15 minutes. Place the red capsicums (bell peppers) on the tray; grill for 15 minutes, turning to blacken all sides. Remove the capsicums (bell peppers) only place in a brown paper bag. Place the mushroom on the baking tray, and grill for 15 minutes.

Remove the mushroom, onion and garlic from the oven. Set the vegetables aside until cool enough to handle.

4. Peel and remove the seeds from the capsicums (bell peppers) place in blender, discarding the seeds and peel. Squeeze the garlic and onion from their skins and add to blender, discarding the skins. Coarsely chop the mushroom and add to the blender along with the remaining olive oil, lemon juice, fennel, tomato sauce (ketchup), and vinegar. Blend until smooth. Season to taste with salt and ground black pepper.

5. Place the shredded lobster meat in the centre of a large bed of salad greens. Pour the dressing around the lobster meat.

Makes 3 to 4 servings

PRAWN AND CRAB SOUP

Crab Soup

INGREDIENTS

170g/6oz can crab meat
   (or fresh, picked crabmeat)

1 egg

4 dried Chinese mushrooms

85g/3oz canned bamboo shoots

1 leek

small piece fresh ginger

1 tablespoon vegetable oil

2 teaspoons soy sauce

1 tablespoon rice wine, mirin or dry sherry

6 cups stock

2 teaspoons salt

freshly ground pepper

1$^{1}/_{2}$ tablespoons cornflour

2 tablespoons chopped parsley

METHOD

1. Drain the crabmeat and break up. Beat the egg in a small bowl.

2. Soak the dried mushrooms in water for 20 minutes, discard the stalks and slice the caps. Drain the bamboo shoots and cut into strips. Slit the leek almost through, discarding the tough green top, wash carefully, then cut into strips. Grate or finely chop the ginger.

3. Heat the oil in a wok or medium-sized saucepan, add the mushrooms, leek, bamboo shoots and ginger and stir-fry for a 1 minute.

4. Add the cra bmeat, sprinkle with soy sauce and rice wine and pour in the heated stock or water. As soon as the liquid comes to the boil, skim off any scum. Season with salt and pepper, stir in the cornflour mixed with a little water, to thicken the soup.

5. Pour in the beaten egg and mix, stirring lightly so that the egg sets in short strands. Sprinkle with finely chopped parsley and serve.

Serves 4–6

Crab Salad with Tomato Dressing

INGREDIENTS

2 large dressed crabs (about 250g/9oz crab meat)

1 large bulb fennel, thinly sliced, and
   feathery top chopped and reserved
   to garnish

85g/3oz mixed salad leaves

1 tablespoon snipped fresh chives
   and paprika or cayenne pepper
   to garnish

Dressing

2 large tomatoes

5 tablespoons olive oil

1 tablespoon white wine vinegar

4 tablespoons single cream

1 teaspoon chopped fresh tarragon

salt and black pepper

pinch of caster sugar

dash of Worcestershire sauce

5cm/2in piece cucumber, diced

METHOD

1. To make the dressing, place the tomatoes in a bowl and cover with boiling water. Leave for 30 seconds, then skin, deseed and cut into small dice. Whisk together the oil and vinegar in a bowl, then whisk in the cream, tarragon and seasoning. Add sugar and Worcestershire sauce to taste, then stir in the tomatoes and cucumber.

2. Mix together the crabmeat and sliced fennel and stir in 4 tablespoons of the dressing. Arrange the salad leaves together with the crab mixture on plates. Spoon over the remaining dressing, then sprinkle with the chives, chopped fennel top and paprika or cayenne pepper.

Serves 4

Fresh Crab with a Mustard-Dressed Salad

INGREDIENTS

4 mignonette lettuces, shredded

3 tablespoons snipped fresh chives

2 dressed crabs

Dressing

2 tablespoons Dijon mustard

2 tablespoons white wine vinegar

6 tablespoons vegetable oil

pinch of sugar

salt and black pepper

METHOD

1. To make the dressing, mix together the mustard, vinegar, oil, sugar and seasoning.

2. Place the lettuce and 2 tablespoons of the chives in a bowl, pour over the dressing and toss well. Arrange in bowls, top with the crab meat and garnish with the remaining chives.

Serves 4

Note: Fresh crab is so good that you don't need to do anything too elaborate with it. Buttered brown bread and this simple salad in a light mustard dressing are all you need.

Hot Crab Salad

INGREDIENTS

2 tablespoons oil

115g/4oz butter

200g/7oz mushrooms, sliced

6 shallots, chopped

1/2 red capsicum, (bell pepper), dice finely

1 cup rice, cooked

115g/4oz water chestnuts, cut in half

2 teaspoons lemon juice

510g/18oz mud-crab meat

salt and cracked black peppercorns

2 tablespoons dried parsley flakes

METHOD

1. Heat the oil and butter in a frying pan, sauté the mushrooms, shallots and capsicum (bell pepper) for 3–5 minutes.

2. Add the rice, mix well, and cook, stirring over moderate heat.

3. Add the water chestnuts, lemon juice and crab meat. Season to taste with salt and pepper.

4. Sprinkle with parsley to serve.

Serves 4–6

FRESH CRAB IN A
MUSTARD-DRESSED SALAD

Thai-style Shellfish and Pomelo Salad

INGREDIENTS

1 pomelo or 2 pink grapefruit

200g/7oz cooked peeled prawns
  (shrimp)

170g/6oz can crab meat in brine,
  drained

1 mignonette lettuce, chopped

1 spring onion (scallion), finely
  chopped

Dressing

1 tablespoon groundnut oil

1 clove garlic, finely chopped

1 shallot, finely chopped

1 red chilli, de-seeded and
  finely chopped

2 tablespoons Thai fish sauce (nam pla)

2 tablespoons soft dark brown sugar

juice of 1 lime

METHOD

1. First make the dressing. Heat the oil in a small frying pan. Fry the garlic, shallot and chilli for 3 minutes or until the garlic has turned pale golden and the shallot has softened. Mix together the fish sauce (nam pla), sugar and lime juice, stir in the shallot mixture, then set aside for 5 minutes to cool.

2. Using a sharp knife, slice off the top and bottom of the pomelo or grapefruit, then remove the skin and pith, following the curve of the fruit. Cut between the membranes to release the segments.

3. Mix the pomelo or grapefruit segments with the prawns (shrimp), crab meat and lettuce. Pour the dressing over and toss, then sprinkle over the spring onion (scallion).

Serves 4

Cajun Crab Salad with Honeydew and Rockmelon

INGREDIENTS

Cajun Mayonnaise

1 medium clove garlic

1 cup mayonnaise

2 tablespoons chopped parsley

1 tablespoon tomato sauce (ketchup)

2 teaspoons drained capers

2 teaspoons hot spicy mustard

2 teaspoons horseradish

1/2 teaspoon dried tarragon

1/2 teaspoon dried oregano

1/4 teaspoon Worcestershire sauce

1/8 teaspoon cayenne pepper

salt

Salad

510g/18oz fresh lump crab meat

1 medium tomato, seeded and
  cut into 5mm/1/4in dice

1/2 cup diced celery

4 green onions, cut into 5mm/1/4 in pieces

1/4 green capsicum (bell pepper), cut into
1/4 in dice

2 tablespoons lime juice

1 small rockmelon, peeled,
  seeded and cut into 12 wedges

1 small honeydew melon, peeled,
  seeded and cut into 12 wedges

12 large lettuce leaves

METHOD

1. For the mayonnaise, mince the garlic and blend in all the remaining ingredients.

2. Combine all the salad ingredients, except the lettuce, with 1/4 cup of the mayonnaise. Arrange 2 lettuce leaves on 6 plates. Place the crab mixture in the centre of the lettuce. Spoon the remaining mayonnaise on the plates and garnish with the melon.

Serves 4

THAI-STYLE SHELLFISH AND POMELO SALAD

Lobster with Dill

INGREDIENTS

2 lobsters weighing approx
   750g/26oz each
few sprigs dill
1 lettuce
2 slices fresh or unsweetened canned
   pineapple
100g/3^{1}/$_{2}$oz button mushrooms
1 tablespoon mayonnaise
200mL/7fl oz whipping cream
pinch sugar
salt and white pepper

METHOD

1. Prepare the lobsters for cooking and add to a very large pan of boiling, slightly salted water. Cook for 15–20 minutes. Drain, take all the meat out of the shells and claws, and dice. Wash and dry the dill and snip off the small feathery leaves, reserving a sprig or 2 for decoration.

2. Wash and dry the lettuce. Drain the pineapple well and cut into small pieces. Slice the mushrooms wafer thin.

3. Place all the ingredients except the lettuce and dill in a bowl and mix with the mayonnaise Fold in the lightly beaten cream, flavoured with a pinch of sugar, salt and freshly ground white pepper.

4. Line a large salad bowl with the lettuce leaves, spoon in the lobster mixture and decorate with the reserved dill sprigs.

Serves 4

Lobster Pineapple Salad

INGREDIENTS

510g/18oz lobster

510g/18oz cooked fish fillets

255g/9oz chopped celery

115g/4oz chopped almonds

370g/13oz pineapple chunks

170g/6oz mayonnaise

1 teaspoon curry powder

$^1/_2$ teaspoon salt

METHOD

1. Dice the lobster, reserving the juice. Break the fish fillets into chunks. Combine the lobster, juice and fish fillets, cover and refrigerate for 10–12 hours.

2. Drain the seafood well and add the remaining ingredients. Toss lighty and serve on a bed of lettuce or hollowed-out pineapple halves.

Serves 6–8

Lobster Bisque

INGREDIENTS

1 small lobster, cooked

1 large carrot, peeled and diced

1 small onion, finely chopped

125g/4^{1}/$_{2}$oz butter

^{3}/$_{4}$ cup dry white wine

bouquet garni (see glossary)

6^{1}/$_{2}$ cups fish or chicken stock

^{3}/$_{4}$ cup rice

salt, pepper and ground cayenne

^{1}/$_{2}$ cup cream

2 tablespoons brandy

chopped parsley

METHOD

1. Split the lobster in half, lengthwise, and remove the flesh from the shell. Set aside. Wrap the shell in an old tea towel, crush the shell with a hammer and set aside. Sauté the carrot and onion in half the butter until softened without colouring (about 5 minutes). Add the crushed shell, sauté a further minute or so then add the wine. Boil hard until reduced by half. Add the bouquet garni, stock and rice.

2. After about 20 minutes, when the rice is tender, remove the large pieces of shell and the bouquet garni. Purée small batches in a food processor with the remainder of the batter, doing so in small batches. Pour through a strainer. Rinse out the food processor to remove every trace of shell and purée the strained liquid again, this time with the lobster flesh, saving a few pieces for the garnish. Reheat gently.

3. Taste, add salt, pepper and cayenne to taste then stir in the cream, brandy and reserved lobster pieces, cut into thin slices. Serve very hot garnished with parsley.

Serves 4

Rock Lobster and Smoked Ocean Trout Salad

INGREDIENTS

1 cooked rock lobster

400g/14oz smoked ocean trout

1 continental cucumber

1 carrot

1 green zucchini (courgette)

1 yellow zucchini (courgette)

100g/3$^{1}/_{2}$ oz tatsoi leaves

1 bunch chives, snipped

Dressing

juice of 2 limes

1 tablespoon palm sugar

$^{1}/_{2}$ cup olive oil

salt and pepper

METHOD

1. Remove the meat from the tail of the rock lobster, slice finely and set aside. Alternatively ask your fishmonger to do this for you. Cut the smoked ocean trout into thin strips and also set aside.

2. Slice the cucumber in half, lengthways and scoop out and discard the seeds. Slice on a mandoline or 'V- slicer' (or use a vegetable peeler) to make long, skinny strips resembling fettuccine. Peel the carrot and slice in the same manner as the cucumber. Keeping the zucchini (courgette) whole, also slice them lengthways into long thin strips.

3. Mix the lobster, ocean trout, vegetables and tatsoi leaves gently.

4. For the dressing, heat the lime juice and dissolve the palm sugar. Pour into a bowl and whisk in the olive oil until the mixture is thick and the oil has emulsified with the lime juice. Season with salt and pepper and mix this through the salad ingredients.

Arrange the salad on an attractive platter and sprinkle the chives over.

Serves 4

Note: Tatsoi is also known as 'spoon cabbage'. It is a leafy Asian green with a slightly spicy cabbage flavour, and is used normally in salads and stir-fries.

Cream of Crab Soup

INGREDIENTS

1 chicken stock (bouillon) cube

1 cup boiling water

1 small onion, chopped

1 tablespoon butter

3 tablespoons flour

$^{1}/_{4}$ teaspoon celery salt

1 teaspoon black pepper

4 cups milk

510g/18oz crab meat

chopped parsley

METHOD

1. Dissolve the stock (boullion) cube in water. Cook the onion in the butter until tender. Blend in the flour and seasonings. Add the milk and stock (bouillion) gradually and cook until thick, stirring constantly. Add the crab meat and heat through. Garnish with parsley.

Serves 4

Salad of Lobster with Raspberries

INGREDIENTS

2 lobster tails, cooked and shells removed

1 small radicchio, leaves separated

1 small mignonette lettuce, leaves separated

115g/4oz snow pea sprouts (mangetout),
   or watercress

1 orange, segmented

255g/9oz strawberries, halved

Dressing

115g/4oz fresh or frozen raspberries

2 tablespoons raspberry vinegar

2 tablespoons vegetable oil

1 teaspoon finely chopped fresh mint

1 tablespoon sugar

METHOD

1. Cut the lobster tails into 1cm/$\frac{1}{2}$in medallions and set aside.

2. Arrange the radicchio, mignonette, sprouts or watercress, lobster, orange segments and strawberries attractively on a serving platter and refrigerate until required.

3. To make the dressing, place the raspberries in a food processor or blender and process until pureed. Push through a sieve to remove the seeds. Combine the raspberry puree with the vinegar, oil, mint and sugar. Mix well to combine, pour over the salad and serve immediately.

Serves 4

Note: Lobster would have to be the undisputed king of shellfish. In this recipe, it is taken to new heights with the addition of a raspberry dressing.

Creamy Lobster Chowder

INGREDIENTS

55g/2oz quick cooking rice

1 teaspoon salt

1/4 teaspoon pepper

1/4 teaspoon paprika

1 tablespoon onion, finely minced

1 small red capsicum (bell pepper), diced

2 stalks celery, chopped

2 cups milk

2 cups light cream

370g/13oz lobster meat, diced

2 tablespoons butter

2 tablespoons parsley, chopped

METHOD

1. Combine the rice, salt, pepper, paprika, onion, capsicum (bell pepper), celery, milk and cream in a saucepan. Cook over medium heat, stirring frequently, for 10–12 minutes, or until the rice softens.

2. Stir in the lobster and butter. Remove from the heat, cool and store in the refrigerator. Just before serving, stir through the parsley then reheat the chowder over medium heat, stirring frequently.

Serves 4–6

Note: This chowder is best 'aged' for at least five hours before serving, so prepare the dish well ahead of time.

Tarragon Seafood Salad

INGREDIENTS

4 tablespoons chopped fresh tarragon

2 tablespoons lime juice

3 teaspoons grated lime rind

1 fresh red chilli, chopped

2 teaspoons olive oil

freshly ground black pepper, to taste

510g/18oz uncooked lobster tail, flesh removed from shell and cut into large pieces or 510g/18oz firm white fish fillets, cut into large pieces

255g/9oz snow pea (mangetout) sprouts or watercress

1 cucumber, sliced into ribbons

2 carrots, sliced into ribbons

1 red capsicum (bell pepper), cut into thin strips

METHOD

1. Place the tarragon, lime juice, lime rind, chilli, oil and black pepper in a bowl and mix to combine. Add lobster, toss to coat and set aside to marinate for 15 minutes.

2. Arrange the snow pea (mangetout) sprouts or watercress, cucumber, carrot and red capsicum (bell pepper) on a large serving platter and set aside.

3. Heat a char-grill or frying pan over a high heat, add the lobster mixture and cook, turning frequently, for 2 minutes or until the lobster is tender. Arrange the lobster over salad, spoon over the pan juices and serve immediately.

Serves 4

Note: To make cucumber and carrot ribbons, use a vegetable peeler to remove strips lengthwise from the cucumber or carrot. This salad is also delicious made using prawns instead of lobster. If using prawns, shell and devein them before marinating.

Spiced Crab Soup

INGREDIENTS

2 cups water

2 tablespoons Denjang paste

1 soft bean curd, in 1cm/$\frac{1}{2}$in cube

1 teaspoon hot red chili powder, mix with 1 tablespoon water

1 slice ginger, size of a dollar coin

1 small onion, sliced

1 garlic clove, crushed

2 crabs, each in 4 pieces

1 zucchini (courgette), sliced

METHOD

1. Put the water and bean paste (denjang) into a pan and simmer over low heat, covered, for 10 minutes. Add the bean curd and cook for 5 minutes more.

2. Now add all the other ingredients and cook for 15 minutes more. Serve in four individual bowls with rice and an assortment of side dishes.

Serves 4

TARRAGON SEAFOOD SALAD

Lobster Rice Salad

INGREDIENTS

170g/6oz lobster meat, diced

510g/18oz cooked rice

1 tablespoon lemon juice

255g/9oz celery, finely diced

55g/2oz green capsicum (bell pepper),
   finely diced

115g/4oz crushed pineapple, drained

1 teaspoon salt

$1/2$ teaspoon black pepper

115mL/4fl oz mayonnaise

METHOD

1. Combine all the ingredients. Place in a bowl or mould. Chill for several hours. Turn out onto a bed of lettuce.

Serves 6

Crab, Mango and Cucumber Salad

INGREDIENTS

455g/16oz fresh lump crab meat, picked
   over for shells and cartilage

20mL/$2/3$fl oz freshly squeezed lime juice

3 tablespoons extra-virgin olive oil

1 tablespoon finely chopped coriander
   (cilantro) leaves, plus 4 whole leaves
   for garnish

2 teaspoons finely chopped mint leaves,
   plus 4 whole leaves for garnish

salt and freshly ground white pepper

hot chilli sauce

1 medium mango, peeled, pitted,
   and cut into 5mm/$1/4$in dice

1 cucumber, peeled, seeded and
   cut into 5mm/$1/4$in dice

1 tablespoon unsalted peanuts,
   toasted and roughly chopped

METHOD

1. Season the crab meat with 1 tablespoon of the lime juice, $1 1/2$ tablespoons of the olive oil, $2/3$ of the chopped coriander (cilantro) and mint, salt and pepper to taste and about 10 drops of hot chilli sauce. Toss the crab meat lightly with a fork or your fingers. If you wish to serve the salad family-style, put the crab in a chilled shallow bowl. For individual servings, arrange the crab in 4 chilled shallow soup plates.

2. Season the mango and cucumber with the remaining lime juice, olive oil, chopped coriander (cilantro) and mint, salt and pepper to taste and about 10 drops of hot chilli sauce. Mix well and scatter the mixture over the crab meat, in either large or small bowls. Sprinkle the salad with the chopped peanuts and top with the whole coriander (cilantro) and mint leaves. Serve mango coulis on the side, if desired.

Serves 4

LOBSTER RICE SALAD

Lobster and Sprout Salad

INGREDIENTS

1$^{1}/_{2}$ cups mayonnaise

$^{1}/_{2}$ cup Pernod

4 large sorrel leaves, finely shredded

$^{1}/_{4}$ cup finely chopped celery

$^{1}/_{4}$ teaspoon chilli sauce

510g/18oz cooked lobster

snow pea (mangetout) sprouts

METHOD

1. Combine the mayonnaise, Pernod, sorrel, celery and chilli sauce. Chop the lobster into bite-size pieces and arrange them on the sprouts. Spoon over the sauce. Serve with thin slices of buttered wholemeal bread.

Serves 4–6

APPETISERS
& SNACKS

Lobster Filo Triangles

INGREDIENTS

8 sheets filo pastry

115g/4oz butter, melted and cooled

Lobster Cream Filling

l cooked lobster

45g/1^1/2oz butter

6 spring onions (scallions), chopped

2 cloves garlic, crushed

1^1/2 tablespoons flour

55mL/2fl oz white wine

55mL/2fl oz double cream

pinch of cayenne pepper

freshly ground black pepper

METHOD

1. To make the filling, remove the meat from the lobster, chop finely and set aside. Melt 45g/1^1/2oz butter in a saucepan over a medium heat, add spring onions (scallions) and garlic and cook, stirring, until the onions are tender. Stir in the flour and cook for 1 minute.

2. Remove the pan from the heat and whisk in the wine and the cream, a little at a time, until well blended. Season to taste with cayenne and black pepper, return to the heat and cook, stirring constantly, until the sauce boils and thickens. Reduce the heat to low and simmer for 3 minutes. Remove from the heat, stir in the lobster meat and cool completely.

3. Cut the pastry sheets lengthwise into 5cm/2in wide strips. Working with one strip of pastry at a time, brush the pastry with melted butter. Place a teaspoonful of the filling on one end of the strip, fold the corner of the pastry diagonally over the filling, then continue folding up the strip to make a neat triangle.

4. Place the triangles on a baking tray, brush with butter and bake in a moderate oven at 180°C/350°F/Gas 4 for 10–15 minutes or until golden.

Makes 24

Note: The scampi, or deep sea lobster as it is also called, is targeted by trawlers mostly off northwestern Australia. They are generally snap-frozen onboard the trawlers; thus making the job of finding fresh specimens a lot more difficult. Scampi has a wonderfully sweet flesh, ideal for sashimi. It is considered by many to have eating qualities above that of the lobster.

Scampi Sashimi

INGREDIENTS

8 scampi or yabbies (if unavailable fresh, frozen is also good)

Chirizu (Spicy Dipping Sauce)
5 teaspoons sake
3 tablespoons freshly grated daikon radish
2 spring onions (scallions), finely sliced
3 tablespoons soy sauce
3 tablespoons lemon juice
1/8 teaspoon hichimi togarashi (seven-pepper spice)

METHOD

1. To prepare the scampi or yabbies, remove the heads and set aside for garnish.

2. Peel back the underside shell from the top down to the tail.

3. Remove the flesh and discard the shells except for the bottom part of tail.

4. Place the scampi meat on a plate, putting the head and tail on as a garnish.

5. To make the dipping sauce, warm the sake in a small saucepan remove it from the heat and quickly ignite it with a match, shaking and shake the pan gently until the flame dies out. Allow to cool.

6. Put the sake with the other ingredients and mix well. Pour into individual bowls and serve with the scampi (or any other sashimi).

Serves 6

Lobster Topping

INGREDIENTS

115g/4oz cream cheese

115mL/4fl oz mayonnaise

55mL/2fl oz sour cream

2 tablespoons lobster juice

2 teaspoons lemon juice

1/2 clove garlic, crushed

1 teaspoon dried chives

255g/9oz lobster meat, diced

METHOD

Beat together the cream cheese, mayonnaise and sour cream. Add the lobster juice, lemon juice, garlic and chives. Beat well. Stir in the lobster. Serve over hot baked potatoes.

Serves 6–8

Crab Meat Soufflé

INGREDIENTS

45g/1¹/₂oz butter

3 tablespoons flour

1 cup milk

salt and freshly ground pepper

pinch of cayenne

170g/6oz can crab meat,
   drained and flaked

¹/₄ cup flaked almonds

4 egg yolks

5 egg whites

METHOD

1. Prepare a 6 cup soufflé mould or four 1 cup or 1¹/₂ cup dishes. Set the oven at 190°C/375°F/Gas 5. Heat a metal tray in the oven.

2. Melt the butter in the saucepan and stir in the flour. Cook over low heat for 1 minute. Gradually add the milk and cook, stirring, until thickened. Season to taste with salt, pepper and cayenne and fold in the crab meat and almonds. Add the egg yolks, one at a time. Whip the egg whites until stiff, then fold into the mixture. Pour into prepared the soufflé dish or dishes, place on a metal tray and bake for about 25 minutes (18 minutes for individual ones) or until puffed and golden.

Serves 4

Devilled Lobster

INGREDIENTS

625g/22oz lobster steamed,
   tail, leg and claw meat separated

¹/₄ teaspoon garlic, minced

¹/₂ tablespoon horseradish, fresh

¹/₂ tablespoon prepared brown mustard

¹/₂ tablespoon lemon juice

1 teaspoon dill weed

¹/₄ teaspoon sweet chilli sauce

³/₄ cup mayonnaise

fresh ground pepper, to taste

18 large eggs, hard-boiled, sliced in
   half and yolks removed

slivered black olives, to garnish

METHOD

1. Cut the lobster meat into small 1cm/¹/₂in chunks. Then place all the ingredients including the egg yolks (with the exception of the white egg halves and olives), in a food processor or blender and blend until slightly smooth.

2. Fill a piping bag with the blended ingredients and squeeze into the egg halves, sprinkle with ground pepper and garnish with the slivered black olives. Refrigerate until ready to use.

Makes 36 as hors d'oevres

CRAB MEAT SOUFFLÉ

Crab-stuffed Mushrooms

INGREDIENTS

8 mushrooms (each about 5cm/2in
   diameter) stem removed
French dressing, for marinating
200g/7oz crab meat
2 tablespoons finely chopped red capsicum
   (bell pepper)
2 tablespoons finely chopped celery
1 teaspoon lemon juice
1/4 teaspoon Dijon Mustard
chopped fresh dill
2 tablespoons sour cream
3 tablespoons mayonnaise

METHOD

1. Marinate the mushrooms in the French
dressing for about 30 minutes.

2. Place the crab meat, capsicum (bell pepper)
and celery in a bowl. Lightly mix together.

3. Blend the remaining ingredients together,
and mix through the crab mixture. Chill.

4. Just before serving, drain the mushroom caps
and fill with the crab mixture.

Serves 4

Crab Meat Ramekins

INGREDIENTS

510g/18oz crab meat
3 rashers bacon
1 teaspoon mustard powder
1 teaspoon ground paprika
1 teaspoon celery salt
2 drops Tabasco sauce
2 tablespoons sweet chilli sauce
1 teaspoon white wine vinegar
1 cup mayonnaise
parsley, for garnish

METHOD

1. Preheat the oven to 180°C/350°F/Gas 4.

2. Divide the crab among 6 greased ramekins and place in the oven to heat through.

3. Chop the bacon, fry until crisp, then sprinkle over the crab.

4. Combine the mustard, paprika, celery salt, Tabasco sauce, chilli sauce, vinegar and mayonnaise.

5. Spoon over the crab meat, and brown under a hot griller until golden. Garnish with chopped parsley.

Serves 4

Lobster Croquettes

INGREDIENTS

510g/18oz lobster meat

$1/2$ teaspoon pepper

$1/2$ teaspoon salt

pinch of mace

115g/4oz breadcrumbs

55g/2oz butter

1 egg, beaten

6 crackers, pulverised

lard, for cooking

chopped parsley, for garnish

METHOD

1. Chop the lobster meat, add pepper, salt and a pinch of mace.

2. Mix with this about a quarter as much breadcrumbs as you have meat. Add enough melted butter to shape them into pointed balls.

3. Roll in the beaten egg, then in the pulverized crackers, and fry in the boiling lard.

4. Serve very hot, garnished with the parsley.

Serves 4

Note: This is a delicious dish for a luncheon or entrée.

Lobster Toasts

INGREDIENTS

255g/9oz cream cheese
55g/2oz unsalted butter
55g/2oz cooked lobster meat
1 tablespoon olive oil
juice of $1/2$ lemon
salt and pepper, to taste
extra olive oil, for serving
12 slices of French baguette,
  or Turkish bread, toasted
fresh parsley, chopped, for garnish

METHOD

1. Combine all the ingredients, except toast and parsley
in a food processor and blend until creamy.

2. Spread on the toast and heat through under
a preheated hot grill before serving.

3. Sprinkle with chopped parsley and ground
black pepper, drizzle with some olive oil and serve.

Serves 6

Crab Meat Fritters

INGREDIENTS

3 eggs

1 cup bean sprouts

3 spring onions (scallions), chopped

400g/14oz crab meat

salt and cracked black peppercorns

oil, for deep frying

Sauce

2 teaspoons cornflour

1 tablespoon sugar

3 tablespoons soy sauce

1 cup chicken stock

2 tablespoons dry sherry

METHOD

1. Beat the eggs in a bowl, stir in the bean sprouts, spring onions (scallions) and crab meat, and add salt and pepper to taste.

2. Heat sufficient oil to cover the base of a frying pan, and drop in all of the crab mixture, a heaped tablespoon at a time.

3. Fry until golden brown on one side, then turn and brown the other side.

4. Remove from the pan and keep warm.

5. For the sauce, blend together the cornflour and sugar in a pan then add the soy sauce and chicken stock.

6. Slowly bring to the boil over a low heat, stirring all the time. Cook for 3 minutes, or until sauce is thickened. Stir in the sherry.

Serves 4

Lobster Cocktail

INGREDIENTS

55g/2oz horseradish

1¹/₂ cups bottled tomato sauce

2 tablespoons fresh lemon juice

2 tablespoons Worcestershire sauce

1 small head iceberg lettuce, outer leaves removed

510g/18oz lobster meat, cut into bite-size pieces

1 lemon, quartered lengthwise

METHOD

1. Make the cocktail sauce by combining the first 4 ingredients in a small bowl. Stir until thoroughly blended, cover with plastic wrap and refrigerate until ready to use.

2. With a sharp knife make clean vertical cuts in the lettuce from top to bottom, thinly slicing the head of the lettuce into loose 'lettuce straw' or chiffonnade.

3. Cover each salad plate or glass soup plate with the sliced lettuce. Spoon 1/4 cup of cocktail sauce into the centre of each lettuce nest. Arrange a quarter of the chilled lobster pieces in a circle around the sauce on each plate. Garnish each dish with a lemon wedge and cocktail fork. Serve immediately.

Serves 4

Scampi with Basil Butter

INGREDIENTS

8 uncooked scampi or yabbies,
** heads removed**

Basil Butter
85g/3oz butter, melted
2 tablespoons chopped fresh basil
1 clove garlic, crushed
2 teaspoons honey

METHOD

1. Cut the scampi or yabbies in half, lengthwise.

2. To make the basil butter, place the butter, basil, garlic and honey in a small bowl and whisk to combine.

3. Brush the cut side of each scampi or yabbie half with basil butter and cook under a preheated hot grill for 2 minutes or until they change colour and are tender.

4. Drizzle with any remaining basil butter and serve immediately.

Serves 4

Sea Captain's Dip

INGREDIENTS

115g/4oz cream cheese
2 tablespoons lemon juice
55mL/2fl oz mayonnaise
¼ teaspoon garlic salt
2 tablespoons onion, diced
1 teaspoon dried chives
170g/6oz lobster meat, finely diced

METHOD

1. Cream the cream cheese and lemon juice. Add the mayonnaise, garlic salt, onion, chives and lobster and mix well.

2. Chill at least for 6 hours, then serve with crackers or fresh vegetables.

Makes 2 cups

Lobster Crêpes

INGREDIENTS

Filling
510g/18oz lobster meat, fresh or frozen

55g/2oz butter

2 tablespoons onion, chopped

455g/16oz mushrooms, sliced

55g/2oz flour

1/2 teaspoon salt

1/6 teaspoon pepper

1 cup milk

55g/2oz butter, melted

55g/2oz Swiss cheese, grated

Crêpes
2 eggs

170g/6oz flour

1/2 teaspoon salt

1 teaspoon dried parsley

1 teaspoon dried chives

1 cup milk

METHOD

1. If frozen, thaw and chop the lobster into bite-sized pieces. Melt the butter and sauté the onions and the mushrooms for 3–5 minutes. Stir in the flour and seasonings, add the milk and cook, stirring constantly until thickened. Add the lobster.

2. To make the crêpes, beat the eggs, add the flour and seasonings. Add the milk and beat until smooth. Refrigerate for 2 hours. For each crêpe, pour 2–3 tablespoons of batter into a heated, oiled pan. Brown lightly on each side.

3. Spoon 3 tablespoons of filling into each crêpe, roll up and arrange in a baking dish. Brush with half the melted butter and sprinkle with the grated cheese. Bake at 220°C/425°F for 5–8 minutes. Stir the remaining melted butter into the remaining filling and serve over the crêpes.

Serves 6

Lobster Puffs

INGREDIENTS

510g/18oz lobster meat

125g/4$^{1}/_{2}$oz cream cheese

1 tablespoon mayonnaise

1/2 tablespoon Worcestershire sauce

1/2 teaspoon salt

1 dash pepper, to taste

1 loaf Italian bread,
   sliced 1cm/1/2 inch thick

METHOD

1. Mix all of the ingredients, except the bread, in a mixing bowl. Remove the crust from each bread slice and then toast. Cut the bread into 5cm/2in triangles, squares and/or round shapes using a biscuit cutter or knife. Lay the bread onto a baking tray or griller pan.

2. Spread the lobster mixture over the bread shapes approximately 5mm/1/4in thick. Place under a griller for 1 minute to brown just before serving. Transfer to a serving dish and enjoy.

Serves 4

LOBSTER CRÊPES

Grilled Scampi with Herb Butter

INGREDIENTS

10–12 scampi
140g/5oz butter
few sprigs fresh herbs, chopped
2 tablespoons chopped parsley
2 cloves garlic, finely chopped
salt and freshly ground pepper

METHOD

1. Split the scampi lengthwise through the centre and arrange, cut side up, on a large shallow dish. Melt the butter and add the herbs and garlic. Drizzle the flavoured butter over the scampi and season with freshly ground pepper. (The scampi can be prepared ahead up to this stage.)

2. Preheat the griller and arrange the scampi, cut side up, on the grilling pan. Cook for about 5 minutes until the flesh has turned white. Remove from the heat, season with salt and arrange on a large serving platter with wedges of lemon. To eat the scampi use a fork to pull out the tail meat.

3. Place a bowl on the table for the discarded shells, and a few finger bowls, each with a squeeze of lemon.

Serves 4

Rice Cakes with Lime Crab

INGREDIENTS

400g/14oz jasmine rice, cooked

30g/1oz fresh coriander (cilantro) leaves, chopped

crushed black peppercorns

vegetable oil, for deep-frying

Lime Crab Topping

170g/6oz canned crab meat, well drained

2 fresh red chillies, seeded and chopped

2 small fresh green chillies, finely sliced

55mL/2fl oz coconut cream

2 tablespoons thick natural yoghurt

3 teaspoons lime juice

3 teaspoons Thai fish sauce (nam pla)

3 teaspoons finely grated lime rind

1 tablespoon crushed black peppercorns

METHOD

1. Combine the rice, coriander (cilantro) and black peppercorns to taste, then press into an oiled 18cm x 28cm/7in x 11in shallow cake tin and refrigerate until set. Cut the rice mixture into 3cm x 4cm/ 1¹/4in x 1¹/2in rectangles.

2. Heat the vegetable oil in a large saucepan until a cube of bread dropped in browns in 50 seconds and cook the rice cakes, a few at a time, for 3 minutes or until golden. Drain on absorbent kitchen paper.

3. To make the topping, place the crab meat, red and green chillies, coconut cream, yoghurt, lime juice and fish sauce in a food processor and process until smooth. Stir in the lime rind and black peppercorns. Serve with warm rice cakes.

Makes 24

Lobster Sashimi

INGREDIENTS

1 whole green (uncooked) lobster

shredded daikon radish

endive, for garnish

shredded carrot, for garnish

METHOD

1. If lobster the is purchased frozen, allow it to defrost overnight in the refrigerator.

2. Remove the head and reserve for garnish.

3. Use poultry scissors to make a nice clean cut in the tail shell.

4. Pull the lobster meat out. Stuff the empty shell with the shredded daikon radish for presentation. Cut the lobster into small sashimi slices.

5. Lay the meat on the daikon-bedded tail. Garnish with the endive and shredded carrot and serve

Serves 4

Note: Traditionally, lobsters that were to be prepared as sashimi were purchased live and killed moments before being presented and served. The Japanese obsession with absolute freshness has made this practice commonplace.

Lobster-stuffed Potatoes

INGREDIENTS

6 potatoes, baked
1 tablespoon butter
115mL/4fl oz sour cream
55g/2oz onion, grated
$1/4$ teaspoon pepper
125g/$4^1/_2$oz lobster meat, diced
55g/2oz mushrooms, diced
115g/4oz Cheddar cheese, grated

METHOD

1. Preheat the oven to 190°C/375°F.

2. Cut the baked potatoes in half the lengthwise and carefully scoop out the insides, reserving the skins.

3. In a bowl, mash the potato, then add the butter, sour cream, onion and pepper. Beat until smooth. Fold in the lobster meat and mushrooms and place the mixture back in the 12 potato skin halves. Sprinkle with the grated cheese and place on a baking tray.

4. Bake for 15–20 minutes, or until the potatoes are heated through.

Serves 6

Lobster Cheese Rolls

INGREDIENTS

115g/4oz celery, chopped
2 tablespoons onion, minced
115mL/4fl oz mayonnaise
1 tablespoon French dressing
115g/4oz Cheddar cheese, grated
85g/3oz slivered almonds, toasted
2 teaspoons lemon juice
1/2 teaspoon salt
6 buttered rolls
510g/18oz cooked lobster meat, sliced

METHOD

1. Combine the first 8 ingredients and toss lightly to combine. Top one half of each roll with the lobster and some celery mixture then cover with the other roll half. Wrap in aluminium foil and place in a preheated 180°C/350°F oven for 8–10 minutes.

Serves 6

Crab Puffs

INGREDIENTS

2 tablespoons butter
2 tablespoons flour
1/2 teaspoon salt
dash of pepper
1 cup milk
2 egg yolks, beaten
1/4 teaspoon paprika
510g/18oz crab meat
1 cup whipping cream
2 egg whites, beaten

METHOD

1. Melt the butter then blend in the flour and seasonings. Add the milk gradually and cook until thick, stirring constantly. Stir a little of the hot sauce into the egg yolks. Add to the remaining sauce, stirring constantly. Add the paprika and crab meat. Whip cream then fold in the egg whites and whipped cream. Place in 6 well greased individual 285mL/10fl oz casserole dishes in a baking dish of hot water. Bake in a preheated moderate 180°C/350°F oven for 40 minutes.

Serves 4

LOBSTER CHEESE ROLLS

Lobster Crowns

INGREDIENTS

24 large mushrooms

$1/4$ teaspoon salt

dash pepper

2 tablespoons butter

1 tablespoon onion, finely diced

2 tablespoons mushroom stems, finely diced

1 teaspoon butter, extra

125g/4$1/2$oz lobster meat, diced

125g/4$1/2$oz Cheddar cheese, grated

METHOD

1. Remove the stems from the mushrooms. Sprinkle the caps with salt and pepper and fry for 5 minutes in butter over medium heat. Combine the onion, mushroom stems, extra butter and lobster. Stuff the caps with the mixture, and sprinkle with grated cheese.

2. Grill for 4–5 minutes.

Serves 4

MAIN MEALS

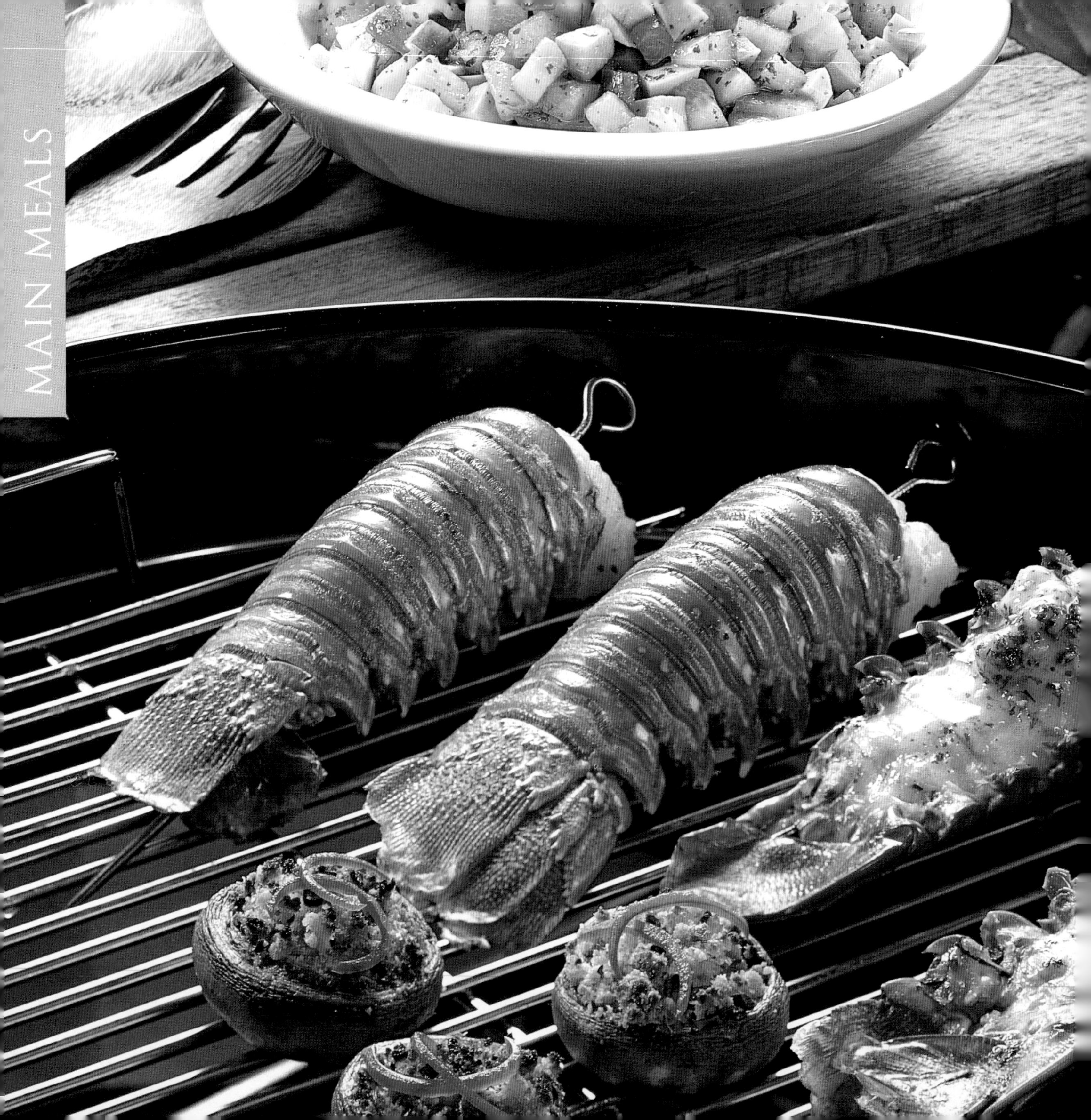

Garlic Lobster Tails with Exotic Salad

INGREDIENTS

6 green (raw) lobster tails

85g/3oz butter, softened

2 teaspoons crushed garlic

2 tablespoons honey and
   lemon marinade (see below)

Exotic Salad

1 avocado, cut into $1/2$ cm/$1/4$in dice

2 Lebanese cucumbers, diced

$1/2$ small rockmelon, peeled and diced

80mL/3fl oz honey and lemon marinade
   (see below)

Honey and Lemon Marinade

115mL/4fl oz olive oil

2 tablespoons lemon juice

1 tablespoon honey

1 tablespoon freshly crushed garlic

2 bay leaves, crushed

METHOD

1. With kitchen scissors, cut each side of the soft shell on the underside of the lobster tails, and remove. Run a metal skewer through the length of each tail to keep them flat while cooking. Soften the butter and mix in the garlic, and honey and lemon marinade. Spread a coating on the lobster meat.

2. Prepare the salad before starting to cook the lobster tails. Mix the diced avocado, cucumber and rockmelon together. Pour the honey and lemon marinade over the salad. Refrigerate until needed.

3. Heat the barbecue to medium-high and oil the grill bars. Place the lobster tails shell-side down and cook until the shell turns red. Spread with more butter and turn meat-side down and cook for 5–8 minutes or until the meat turns white. Turn again and cook for 2 minutes more, shell-side down. Remove the skewers and place the lobster on warm plates. Dot with any remaining butter mixture and serve immediately with exotic salad.

Serves 4–6

Grilled Lobster with Chilli Salsa

INGREDIENTS

2 cooked lobsters (about 340g/12oz each)

4 teaspoons olive oil

cayenne pepper

Salsa

2 tablespoons olive oil

**1 red capsicum (bell pepper),
de-seeded and diced**

1 small onion, chopped

**1 large red chilli, de-seeded
and finely chopped**

1 tablespoon sun-dried tomato paste

salt and black pepper

METHOD

1. To make the salsa, heat the oil in a saucepan and fry the red capsicum (bell pepper), onion and chilli for 5 minutes or until tender. Stir in the tomato paste and season to taste. Transfer to a bowl.

2. To cut the lobsters in half lengthways, and turn one on its back. Cut through the head end first, using a large, sharp knife, then turn the lobster around and cut through the tail end. Discard the small greyish 'sac' in the head – everything else in the shell is edible. Crack the large claws with a small hammer or wooden rolling pin. Repeat with the second lobster. Drizzle the cut side of the lobsters with the oil and sprinkle with the cayenne pepper.

3. Heat a large non-stick frying pan or ridged cast iron grill pan until very hot, then add the lobster halves, cut-side down, and cook for 2–3 minutes, until lightly golden. Serve with the salsa.

Serves 2

Lobster Abegweit

INGREDIENTS

3 tablespoons butter

510g/18oz lobster meat, diced

255g/9oz mushrooms, sliced

1 tablespoon onion, diced

3 tablespoons flour

1 teaspoon salt

370g/13oz evaporated milk

1/2 cup whole milk

55g/2oz processed cheese spread

2 tablespoons parsley, chopped

pasta of choice, cooked

METHOD

1. Melt the butter, add the lobster meat and sauté for 5 minutes. Add the mushrooms and onion, and sauté an additional 5 minutes. Stir in the flour, salt, evaporated milk and whole milk. Cook, stirring constantly until thick and smooth. Stir in the cheese spread and parsley.

2. Toss through hot cooked pasta and serve.

Serves 6

Cognac Lobster with Basil Butter

INGREDIENTS

900g/32oz uncooked lobsters,
   halved and cleaned

2 tablespoons lemon juice

2 tablespoons olive oil

freshly ground black pepper

Basil Butter

115g/4oz butter, roughly chopped

2 tablespoons finely chopped
   fresh basil leaves

2 teaspoons finely chopped fresh parsley

freshly ground black pepper

3 tablespoons cognac

METHOD

1. To make the basil butter, beat the butter until smooth. Stir in the basil and parsley and season to taste with black pepper. Place in a small bowl and refrigerate until required.

2. Drizzle the lobsters with lemon juice and brush the flesh with oil. Cook under a hot grill or on a barbecue, shell-side first, for 5 minutes. Turn over and cook for 5–10 minutes, or until the flesh is just cooked. Brush with extra oil, if necessary, during cooking.

3. Remove the lobsters from the heat. Remove the flesh from the tails in one piece and cut into pieces. Pile back into the shells and set aside to keep warm. Warm the cognac, hold a lighted match over it. As soon. As it ignites spoon over the lobster.

4. Divide the butter into 4 portions and place one piece on each lobster half.

Serves 4

LOBSTER ABEGWEIT

Crab in Creamy Tomato Sauce

INGREDIENTS

30g/1oz butter

225g/8oz cherry tomatoes

6 spring onions (scallions), chopped

3 teaspoons freshly crushed garlic

1kg/35oz crab meat

140g/5oz fresh parsley, chopped

2 tablespoons lemon juice

2 tablespoons tomato paste

1 cup cream

salt and pepper

pasta of choice, cooked

METHOD

1. Melt the butter in a frying pan. Add the cherry tomatoes, spring onion (scallions) and garlic and sauté for 3 minutes. Reduce the heat to low, stir in the crab meat, and parsley, and cook over low heat for 2 minutes.

2. Stir in the lemon juice, tomato paste and cream. Season with salt and pepper. Heat gently.

3. Serve over hot cooked pasta

Serves 4–6

Crab Casserole

INGREDIENTS

20g/^{2}/$_3$oz butter

1 onion, chopped

1 green capsicum (bell pepper), diced

400g/14oz crab meat

200mL/7fl oz mayonnaise

4 hard-boiled eggs, chopped

255g/9oz cooked rice

1^1/$_2$ cups fresh bread, cut into cubes

1 tablespoon parsley flakes

55mL/2fl oz butter, melted

METHOD

1. Preheat the oven to 180°C/350°F/Gas 4.

2. Heat the butter in a pan, add the onion and capsicum (bell pepper), and stir over a moderate heat, until the onions are soft.

3. Stir in the crab, mayonnaise, eggs and rice.

4. Spoon the mixture into an ovenproof dish. Mix together the bread cubes, parsley and melted butter.

5. Sprinkle the breadcrumb mix over the crab mixture. Bake in a moderate oven for 20–25 minutes.

Serves 4

Bouillabaisse

INGREDIENTS

**3kg/6^1/$_2$ lb mixed fish and seafood,
including firm white fish fillets, prawns
(shrimp), mussels, crab and calamari
(squid) rings**

55mL/2fl oz olive oil

2 cloves garlic, crushed

2 large onions, chopped

2 leeks, sliced

**2 x 400g/14oz canned tomatoes,
undrained and mashed**

**1 tablespoon chopped fresh thyme
or 1 teaspoon dried thyme**

**2 tablespoons chopped fresh basil
or 1^1/$_2$ teaspoons dried basil**

2 tablespoons chopped fresh parsley

2 bay leaves

2 tablespoons finely grated orange rind

1 teaspoon saffron threads

1 cup dry white wine

1 cup fish stock

freshly ground black pepper

METHOD

1. Remove the bones and skin from the fish fillets and cut into 2cm/^{3}/$_4$in cubes. Peel and devein the prawns (shrimp), leaving the tails intact. Scrub and remove the beards from the mussels. Cut the crab into quarters. Set aside.

2. Heat the oil in a large saucepan over a medium heat, add the garlic, onions and leeks and cook for 5 minutes or until the onions are golden. Add the tomatoes, thyme, basil, parsley, bay leaves, orange rind, saffron, wine and stock and bring to the boil. Reduce the heat and simmer for 30 minutes.

3. Add the fish and crab and cook for 10 minutes. Add the remaining seafood and cook for 5 minutes longer or until the fish and seafood are cooked. Season to taste with black pepper.

Serves 6

Crab with Ginger

INGREDIENTS

2 x 750g/26oz or 1 x 1.5kg/3^{1}/3lb
   fresh mud crab
1 tablespoon corn oil
55g/2oz fresh peeled ginger, thinly
   sliced and cut into strips
1 teaspoon crushed garlic
5 shallots, cut into 5cm/2in pieces
1 cup fish stock
1 tablespoon dry sherry
1 teaspoon oyster sauce
^{1}/2 teaspoon Worcestershire sauce
1 tablespoon soy sauce
^{1}/2 teaspoon sugar
2 teaspoon cornflour, mixed with
   1 tablespoon cold water
1 teaspoon sesame oil
1 red chilli, slivered, for garnish
boiled rice, for serving

METHOD

1. Steam the crab for 8 minutes over vigorously boiling water. Remove the crab, let cool, then remove the top shell and clean. Cut the body in half and remove the legs and claws. Set aside.

2. Preheat a wok or large skillet, then heat the oil, add ginger and stir-fry until the ginger is fragrant (about 30 seconds).

3. Add the garlic and shallots with the crab pieces, and stir-fry for about 1 minute.

4. Combine the stock, sherry, oyster sauce, Worcestershire sauce, soy sauce and sugar, and pour into the wok. Cover and cook over medium heat for 3 minutes.

5. Remove the crab with tongs, and set aside on plate.

6. Add the dissolved cornflour to the wok and cook, stirring, until the sauce thickens (about 1 minute).

7. Pour the sauce and shallot mixture onto a serving platter, reassemble the crab, and place the shell over the body to give the impression of a whole crab lying on the platter.

8. Trickle sesame oil over the surface, garnish with chilli slivers, and serve with boiled rice on the side.

Serves 4

Grilled Lobster With Lemon-Chervil Butter

INGREDIENTS

14 cups water
2 teaspoons salt
2 x ^{1}/2–^{3}/4kg/1–1^{1}/4 lb live lobsters
6 tablespoons butter, unsalted
4 tablespoons fresh lemon juice
8 sprigs chervil, leaves only, chopped
   (or substitute parsley)
1 teaspoon mixed herbs
1 lemon, quartered lengthwise

METHOD

1. In an 7–9L/8–10qt stock pot over high heat, bring salted water to a rolling boil. Blanch the lobsters for 3 minutes. Immediately remove and chill in a large bowl filled with ice and water. In a 2–3 of minutes, when the lobsters have cooled enough to handle easily, place them on their backs on a cutting board. With a large sharp kitchen knife or cleaver, cut each lobster lengthwise into two separate halves. Remove the intestinal tract from the tails, and rinse the halves under cold water to remove the tomalley (soft green liver). Crack each claw and remove the meat.

Cut the claw meat into bite-size portions and place it in the split body cavity.

2. In a small saucepan, melt the butter slowly over a low heat, being careful not to let the butter brown. Add the lemon juice, chervil and mixed herbs. Stir to blend thoroughly and brush the mixture liberally onto the exposed meat of both lobster halves.

3. With the griller set on high, cook the lobster halves until the meat is opaque and nicely grilled, (approximately 5 minutes). Serve immediately with fresh lemon wedges and remaining lemon chervil butter for dipping.

Serves 4

CRAB WITH GINGER

Devilled Crab Bake

INGREDIENTS

200g/7oz can crab meat

55g/2oz butter

2 onions, chopped

2 red capsicum (bell pepper), chopped

2 sticks celery, sliced

3 cloves garlic, crushed

1/2 cup mayonnaise

1 tablespoon Worcestershire sauce

2 tablespoons fruit chutney

2 tablespoons chopped parsley

1/2 cup fresh white breadcrumbs

30g/1oz butter, extra

1/4 teaspoon paprika

METHOD

1. Drain and flake crab meat. Melt the butter in a frying pan, add the onion, capsicum (bell pepper), celery and garlic and stir over low heat until the vegetables are tender.

2. Stir in the crab, mayonnaise, Worcestershire sauce, chutney and parsley. Spoon into four 1 cup serving dishes.

3. Combine the breadcrumbs, melted butter and paprika, sprinkle over the crab mixture and bake in a moderate oven for 15 minutes or until golden brown and heated through.

Serves 4

Crab Strudel

INGREDIENTS

55g/2oz shallots, diced

2 cups mushrooms, sliced

55g/2oz onions, diced

55mL/2fl oz melted butter

1 1/3 kg/3lb lump crab meat

2 teaspoons garlic, minced

1 teaspoon thyme

1 teaspoon oregano

salt and pepper, to taste

455g/16oz cream cheese

55g/2oz Parmesan cheese

55mL/2fl oz double cream

6 sheets filo pastry

METHOD

1. Sauté the shallots, mushrooms and onions in the clarified butter. Add the crab meat, garlic, herbs, seasoning and cheese. Cool down with the double cream. Spoon into individual 1cup casserole dishes and top with filo pastry. Brown in a preheated oven at 180°C/350°F/Gas 4 for 7 1/2 minutes.

Serves 5

DEVILLED CRAB BAKE

Sherried Crab Vol-au-Vents

INGREDIENTS

255g/9oz mushrooms

3 tablespoons butter

2 tablespoons butter, extra

3 tablespoons flour

1 cup chicken stock

115mL/4fl oz cream

510g/18oz crab meat, flaked

55g/2oz Parmesan cheese

55g/2oz baby spinach leaves

1/2 red capsicum (bell pepper), finely diced

salt and cracked black peppercorns

2 tablespoons dry sherry

vol-au-vent cases

METHOD

1. Sauté the mushrooms in 2 tablespoons the butter, and set aside.

2. Melt the extra butter and stir in the flour. Cook, stirring, for 2 minutes.

3. Over low heat stir in the chicken stock and cream. When the sauce is boiling, add the crab meat and mushrooms.

4. When the sauce comes to the second boil, add the Parmesan cheese, spinach and capsicum (bell pepper) and season with salt and pepper.

5. Remove from the heat and add the sherry. Spoon into heated vol-au-vent cases.

Serves 4–6

Crab-stuffed Eggplant

INGREDIENTS

3 whole eggplants (aubergine), medium

2 medium onions, finely chopped

3 cloves garlic, finely chopped

1 stalk of celery, finely chopped

2 capsicum (bell peppers), chopped

155g/4oz butter

salt and pepper, to taste

255g/9oz medium prawns (shrimp), peeled

255g/9oz lump crab meat

55g/2oz parsley, chopped

1 teaspoon paprika

155g/4oz breadcrumbs

2 teaspoons olive oil

METHOD

1. Place the whole eggplants (aubergine) in large pot with enough water to cover the them. Simmer the eggplant (aubergine) until are soft. Remove from heat and place in iced water. When cool cut the eggplants (aubergine) in half and scrape the flesh out. Be careful not to tear the skin. Next sauté onions, garlic, celery and capsicum (bell pepper) in butter until soft. Add the eggplant (aubergine) flesh that you scraped out and salt and pepper and cook until all the liquid has evaporated. Add the prawns (shrimp) and cook about for 5 minutes.

2. Turn the heat off and fold in the crab meat, parsley, paprika and enough breadcrumbs to give the mixture a, thick paste consistency. Fill the empty shells with the mixture and lightly spread the remaining breadcrumbs on top and sprinkle the olive oil on top of each half eggplant (aubergine). Bake in a preheated oven at 180°C/350°F/Gas 4 for about 25 minutes.

Serves 6

SHERRIED CRAB VOL-AU-VENTS

Crab au Gratin

INGREDIENTS

4 small crabs
1 tablespoon chopped shallots
1/2 cup chopped mushrooms
1 tablespoon butter or margarine
2 tablespoons cognac
salt and pepper to taste

Gratin Sauce
2 tablespoons butter or margarine
2 tablespoons flour
1 1/2 cups fish stock

1/2 cup cream
1 teaspoon French mustard
1 teaspoon cayenne pepper
1/2 cup grated cheese

METHOD

1. Prepare the crab meat in the usual way and set to one side, being careful to keep the shells intact. Sauté the shallots and mushrooms in the butter, season and pour over the warmed ignited cognac. Remove from the heat.

2. Make the sauce by melting the butter in a saucepan and stirring in the flour over a low heat for 1–2 minutes. Gradually add the fish stock and stir until the sauce thickens then stir in the cream, mustard and seasoning.

3. Allow to simmer for 2–3 minutes then remove from the heat and stir in the crab meat and mushrooms. Spoon the mixture into the crab shells, sprinkle with cheese and bake at 165°C/330°F/Gas 3 for 5 minutes.

Serves 4

Grilled Lobster with Lemon-Lime Butter

INGREDIENTS

4 live lobsters (each 680g/1 1/2 lb)
115g/4oz salted butter
1/4 cup chopped fresh coriander (cilantro)
1 fresh lemon, juice of
1 fresh lime. juice of
lemon and lime wedges and coriander
**   (cilantro) sprigs, for garnish**

METHOD

1. Bring a large pot of water to a rolling boil over high heat. Plunge the lobsters headfirst into the water and cook for 5 minutes, or until bright red. Remove the lobsters and plunge into a large bowl of cold water to stop the cooking.

Drain in a colander. Refrigerate if you do not plan to grill right away.

2. Prepare the lemon-lime butter. Melt the butter in a small saucepan over medium heat. Remove from the heat and stir in the coriander (cilantro) and lemon and lime juice. Set aside.

3. Preheat the grill to high and brush with oil.

4. Place a lobster on its back on a cutting board. Using a large sharp knife split the lobster down the middle, being careful not to cut completely through the shell. Remove the black vein from the tail, the tomalley (soft green liver) from the body and the sand sac located near the head. Repeat with the

remaining lobsters. Baste the lobster meat with some of the lemon-lime butter.

5. Grill the lobsters flesh-side down for 5–6 minutes, or until the flesh is just beginning to look opaque. Turn the lobsters over, baste with more lemon-lime butter and continue to cook for 4–5 minutes longer, or until the lobsters are cooked through. Transfer the lobsters to a large warm platter and garnish with lemon and lime wedges and coriander (cilantro) sprigs. Transfer the remaining lemon-lime butter to a small dipping dish and serve separately.

Serves 4

CRAB AU GRATIN

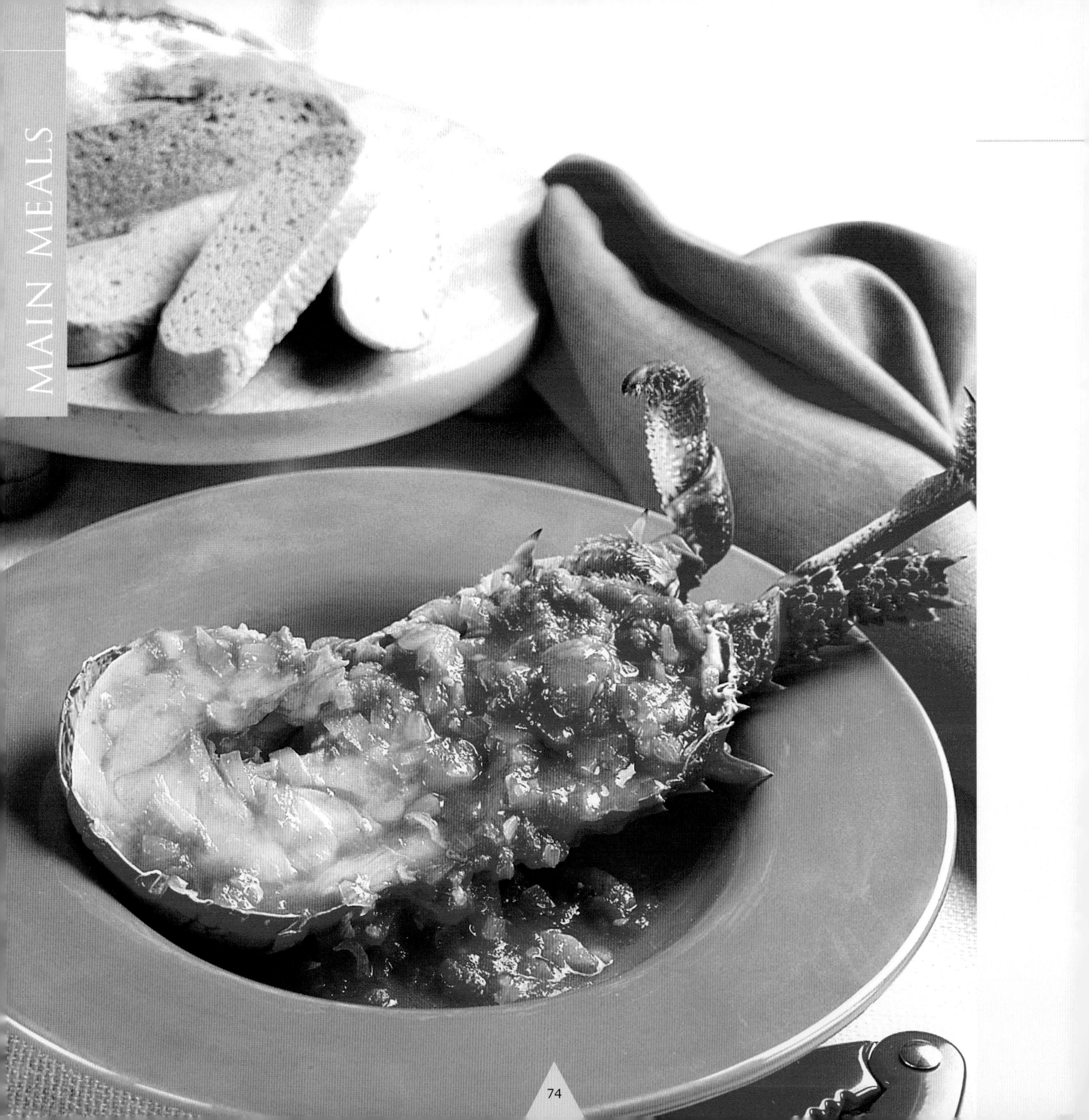

Lobster Sweet and Sour

INGREDIENTS

2 cups dry white wine

2 carrots

2 celery stalks

1 onion

1 bouquet garni (see glossary)

$1^1/_2$ teaspoons coarse sea salt

black peppercorns

4 cups water

1 lobster weighing 1kg/$2^1/_4$lb

2 shallots

45g/$1^1/_2$ oz butter

3 tablespoons olive oil

200mL/7fl oz sparkling white wine

400g/14oz ripe tomatoes

salt and pepper, to season

1 teaspoon sugar

METHOD

1. Make the court bouillon, in which to cook the lobster, with the white wine, all the vegetables except the shallots (prepared and cut in pieces), the bouquet garni, $1^1/_2$ teaspoons coarse sea salt, a few peppercorns and the water. Prepare the lobster, add to the boiling court bouillon and cook gently for about 30 minutes. Drain well and when slightly cooler, cut lengthwise down the middle. Remove the flesh carefully, reserving the shells.

2. Peel and finely chop the shallots and fry in the butter and 3 tablespoons of oil. Add the sparkling wine and reduce by half. Blanch, peel and seed the tomatoes, chop and add to the pan. Boil for 10 minutes, uncovered, to reduce and thicken, and season with salt and pepper. Add the sugar, simmer for 10 minutes more, then add the lobster flesh (still in 2 halves). Stir gently while cooking in the sauce for 5 minutes.

3. Use 2 slotted fish slices or similar to remove the lobster halves from the sauce and replace the lobster in the half shells on a heated serving plate. Coat them with a little sauce and serve the rest in a sauce boat. Serve with a mixed salad

Serves 2

Surf and Turf

INGREDIENTS

2 porterhouse steaks

2 tablespoons butter

2 cloves garlic, finely chopped

1 large lobster tail

1 tablespoon chopped parsley

METHOD

1. Place the steaks on hot grill and cook to your liking. Remove to heated serving plates and keep warm.

2. Heat the butter in a frying pan and cook the garlic for 1–2 minutes. Carefully remove the shell from lobster tail and cut the flesh into pieces. Add the lobster and parsley to the pan and cook for 3–4 minutes over a medium high heat.

3. Spoon the lobster and butter over each steak and serve with grilled asparagus.

Serves 2

Lobster Flambé

INGREDIENTS

2 lobsters weighing approximately
  625g/1¹/₄lb each
3 tablespoons brandy
salt and freshly ground black pepper
butter

METHOD

1. Rinse the lobsters under cold running water, dry with kitchen paper and cut lengthwise in half, using a strong, heavy kitchen knife.

2. Remove the sand sac in the head and the black thread running down the back (the intestinal tract). Season with salt and freshly ground pepper and generously brush all over the cut surface with melted butter.

3. Place on a very hot serving plate, heat 3 tablespoons of brandy, pour over the lobsters and set alight. Place on the table while still flaming.

Serves 4

Lobster Bordelaise

INGREDIENTS

1 lobster weighing 1kg/2^1/$_4$ lb

2 tablespoons olive oil

55g/2oz butter

55mL/2fl oz good brandy

1 onion, finely chopped

1 carrot, finely chopped

1 small white celery heart, finely chopped

2 cloves garlic, crushed

2 shallots, finely chopped

1^1/$_2$ cups good red wine

2 tablespoons tomato paste

1 bouquet garni (see glossary)

salt

freshly ground black pepper

few sprigs parsley, chopped

8 triangles white bread

METHOD

1. A live lobster is traditional for this dish. Use a cleaver or sharp, heavy kitchen knife to cut off the head and slice the body into 'steaks', cutting through the shell where the rings are jointed together. Remove and discard the black intestinal tract and the sand sac or stomach (found in the head). Crush the thin legs, collecting the juice which runs out and place in a bowl, together with the liver. Reserve the coral if you have a hen (female) lobster.

2. Heat 2 tablespoons of oil in a large, deep pan with 30g/1oz butter, add the slices of lobster (still in the shell) and fry briskly until the shell is red. Transfer to a very hot flameproof dish, pour the heated brandy over, and flame.

3. Add the vegetables to the oil, butter and juices left in the pan and fry gently until tender. Pour in the wine, the juice from the lobster, the tomato paste, bouquet garni, salt and freshly ground pepper. Simmer for 15 minutes then discard the bouquet garni and liquidise the sauce. Return to the pan and add the lobster pieces. Cook gently for 10 minutes. Weight the coral if present, then weigh out an equal amount of butter softened at room temperature and work the coral into it. Add 2 tablespoons of the sauce from the pan and mix well, then stir into the saucepan. Cook over the lowest possible heat for 10 minutes more.

4. Serve the lobster pieces coated with the sauce and sprinkled with parsley, surrounded by small triangles or shapes of bread the toasted or lightly fried in butter.

Serves 4

Fresh Crab Tagliatelle

INGREDIENTS

340g/12oz dried tagliatelle

3 tablespoons olive oil

2 cloves garlic, chopped

1 red chilli, de-seeded and chopped

finely grated rind of 1 lemon

2 fresh dressed crabs, to give
    about 315g/ 11oz crab meat

200mL/7fl oz single cream

1 tablespoon lemon juice

salt and black pepper

2 tablespoons chopped
    fresh parsley, to garnish

METHOD

1. Cook the pasta according to the instructions on the packet, until tender but still firm to the bite, then drain.

2. Meanwhile, heat the oil in a large heavy-based frying pan and gently fry the garlic, chilli and lemon rind for 3–4 minutes, until softened but not browned. Add the crab meat, cream and lemon juice and simmer for 1–2 minutes to heat through. Season to taste.

3. Transfer the pasta to serving bowls. Spoon the crab mixture over the top and sprinkle with the parsley to garnish.

Serves 4

Grilled Rock Lobster

INGREDIENTS

2 x 285g/10oz rock lobster tails, thawed

1 teaspoon salt

1 teaspoon paprika

1/8 teaspoon white pepper

1/8 teaspoon garlic powder

1/2 cup olive oil

1 tablespoon lemon juice

METHOD

1. Split the rock lobster tails lengthwise with a large knife.

2. To make the marinade, mix the seasoning with oil and lemon juice.

3. Brush the meat side of tail with the marinade.

4. Pre heat a grill and place the rock lobster tails meat-side down and grill for 5–6 minutes until well scored.

5. Turn the rock lobster and cook for another 6 minutes, brushing often with the remaining marinade.

6. The lobster is done when it is opaque and firm to the touch.

Serves 2

FRESH CRAB TAGLIATELLE

Lobster with Apples and Calvados

INGREDIENTS

3 apples

1 small carrot, chopped into small pieces

1 leek, cut into rings

1 small onion, coarsely chopped

6 cups dry apple cider

salt and pepper

1 lobster weighing approx 1kg/2$^{1}/_{4}$lb

2 tablespoons sultanas, soaked in water

3 tablespoons double cream

1$^{1}/_{2}$ tablespoons calvados

55g/2oz unsalted butter

METHOD

1. Use a firm variety of apple that will not disintegrate when cooked. Place the carrot, leek and onion in a deep, non-metallic saucepan. Remove the core from one apple but do not peel, cut into small pieces and add to the saucepan. Add all but 100mL/3$^{1}/_{2}$fl oz of the cider and season with salt and a little freshly ground white or black pepper.

2. Bring to the boil and boil for 2 minutes. If you are using a live lobster, add it to the fast boiling liquid now. Cover and cook for 10 minutes.

3. Peel, core and thinly slice the remaining apples and use to cover the bottom of a wide, shallow ovenproof dish. Sprinkle with the well drained sultanas. Spoon half the cream and the remaining cider over the apples. Place in the oven, preheated to 200°C/400°F, uncovered, for 10 minutes.

4. Drain the lobster. Boil the cider stock fast until reduced to about 600mL/21fl oz. Draw aside from the heat and when it has cooled a little, liquidise until smooth. Return to the saucepan to the heat with the rest of the cream and the calvados and boil over a moderate heat until it has reduced further and thickened slightly. Remove from heat. Beat in the butter, a small piece at a time. Add salt and freshly ground pepper to taste.

5. If you have cooked the lobster in the cider, cut in half lengthwise at this point. If you have bought your lobster ready-cooked, place cut sides down on top of the apple slices for their last 5 minutes baking in the oven to warm through and take up a little of the apple and cider flavour. Remove and discard the small legs and antennae, the stomach sac, spongy gills and intestinal tract. Place each half on a heated plate, arrange the baked apple slices and sultanas on top and coat with the sauce.

Serves 2 generously

Chilli Crab

INGREDIENTS

2 medium or 1 large crab,
   or 6 blue swimmer crabs
3 tablespoons vegetable oil
1 tablespoon lemon juice
salt

Sauce

2–3 red chillies, seeded and chopped
1 onion, peeled and chopped
2 cloves garlic, peeled and chopped
2 teaspoons grated fresh ginger
2 tablespoons vegetable oil
2 ripe tomatoes, skinned, seeded and
   chopped, or 2 teaspoons tomato paste
1 teaspoon sugar
1 tablespoon light soy sauce
3 tablespoons water

METHOD

1. Clean the crabs thoroughly, then cut each body into 2 or 4 pieces. Chop or crack the claws into 2 or 3 places if they are large. Heat the oil in a frying pan, add the crab pieces and fry for 5 minutes, stirring constantly. Add the lemon juice and salt to taste, remove from the heat and keep hot.

2. To make the sauce, put the chillies, onion and garlic with ginger in a blender and work to a smooth paste. Heat the oil in a wok or a deep frying pan. Add the spice paste and fry for 1 minute, stirring constantly. Add the tomatoes, sugar and soy sauce and stir-fry for 2 minutes, then stir in the water. Add salt if necessary and simmer for a further 1 minute. Add the crab and stir to coat each piece in the sauce and cook the crab through, only a minute or two. Serve hot.

Serves 4

Note: If using live crabs, the best way to handle them is to wrap them in paper and put in the freezer long enough to numb them. Then pierce and cut through eyes and shell, or with a heavy cleaver cut quickly in two.

Lobster and Scallop Supreme

INGREDIENTS

2 cups rice

1kg/2¹/₄lb lobster

3 tablespoons butter or margarine

2 tablespoons lemon juice

680g/24oz scallops

6 shallots, chopped

1 tablespoon chopped parsley

METHOD

1. Cook the rice in boiling salted water for 12–15 minutes. Drain and keep warm. Halve the lobster lengthwise and remove the digestive tract. Chop the flesh into bite size pieces.

2. Melt 1 tablespoon of the butter in a frying pan with the lemon juice and sauté the scallops and shallots until just tender. Add the lobster and allow to heat through.

3. Toss the parsley and remaining butter through the rice and spoon onto a heated serving plate. Spoon the seafood mixture into the shells and serve with the rice.

Serves 4

Baked Crab and Prawns

INGREDIENTS

510g/18oz crab meat

510g/18oz prawns (shrimp), cooked

115g/4oz shallots, chopped

115g/4oz red capsicum (bell pepper),
   chopped

115g/4oz celery, chopped

4 tablespoons lemon juice

3 tablespoons sweet chilli sauce

1 cup mayonnaise

buttered bread crumbs

METHOD

1. Preheat the oven to 180°C/350°F/Gas 4.

2. Combine all the ingredients, except breadcrumbs in a greased casserole dish. Top the with buttered breadcrumbs.

3. Cook in a moderate oven for 25–30 minutes, or until bubbly-hot.

Serves 4–6

Lobster Alfredo

INGREDIENTS

1 tablespoon butter

$1/2$ cup lobster fumet (fish stock)

2 cups double cream

310g/11oz freshly grated Parmesan cheese

dash of Worcestershire sauce

$1/4$ teaspoon Tabasco sauce

$1/4$ teaspoon black pepper

1 teaspoon Dijon mustard

340g/12oz fettucine pasta

255g/9oz fresh lobster meat

4 egg yolks

55g/2oz fresh chopped parsley

METHOD

1. Over medium heat, in a medium-sized saucepan, melt the whole butter and add the lobster fumet and double cream and turn the heat up to medium high.

2. When the cream is hot, just before boiling, add the Parmesan cheese and whisk briskly until all the cheese is melted and dissolved into the cream.

3. Add the Worcestershire, Tabasco, black pepper and Dijon and whisk thoroughly again. Reduce the heat again to a fast simmer and allow the mixture to simmer for 20 minutes.

4. While the sauce is simmering, cook the pasta to your liking, drain and set onto plates. Cut the lobster meat into small pieces and add to the sauce. Add the egg yolks and turn the heat to medium-high. The sauce should be of medium thickness. Ladle the sauce over the pasta, sprinkle with the fresh chopped parsley and serve.

Serves 4

BAKED CRAB
& PRAWNS

Sake-simmered Lobster

INGREDIENTS

2 live lobsters, about 455g/1 lb each

2 leeks, cut into rounds

115g/4oz watercress

8–10cm/3–4in fresh ginger (45g/1^{1}/$_{2}$oz)

1 tablespoon fresh ginger juice

chervil leaves

For Simmering

2 cups sake

^{1}/$_{2}$ cup water

7 tablespoons mirin

2 tablespoons dark soy sauce

2 tablespoons light soy sauce

2 tablespoons sugar

^{1}/$_{2}$ teaspoon salt

METHOD

1. Cut the live lobsters in half lengthwise and then cut each half into 2–3 pieces.

2. Cut the leeks into 1^{1}/$_{2}$cm/^{3}/$_{4}$in rounds, boil in salted water until just tender and drain.

3. Blanch the watercress in lightly salted boiling water, drain and refresh in cold water. Drain again and cut into 4cm/1^{1}/$_{2}$in lengths.

4. Slice the ginger with the grain into very fine slivers and soak in cold water for 2–3 minutes.

5. Place the sake and water in a pan and bring to the boil over high heat, then add all the remaining simmering ingredients. Add the lobster and cover with a plate which fits down inside the pan and sits directly onto the food (this ensures even heat and flavour distribution by forcing the rising heat down). Boil for 5–6 minutes over high heat until the meat can be easily removed from the shell. Ladle the simmering liquid over the lobster several times. Add the leek and watercress. Heat through, add the ginger juice and immediately remove from the heat.

6. Divide the lobster and vegetables among 4 bowls. Pour in an ample amount of sauce. Top with well drained ginger, garnish with chervil and serve.

Serves 4

SAKE-SIMMERED LOBSTER

Lobster with Lemon and Dill Sauce

INGREDIENTS

4 green lobster tails

85g/3oz butter

1 large clove garlic, crushed

1/2 cup sherry

2 tablespoons fresh dill, chopped

145mL/5fl oz fish stock

310mL/11fl oz cream

1 dessertspoon tomato paste

salt, to taste

freshly ground black pepper

juice of 1/2 lemon

510g/18oz spaghetti No. 3, boiled
   and drained

extra fresh dill, chopped

METHOD

1. Remove the lobster meat from the shell and cut into medallions.

2. Melt the butter and sauté the garlic. Quickly add the lobster and sauté briskly. Set aside and keep warm.

3. Now add the sherry and dill to the pan and reduce the liquid by half. Add the fish stock, again reducing by half. Turn heat to medium and add the cream, tomato paste, salt and pepper and simmer for approximately 5 minutes.

4. Return the lobster meat to the pan together with its juices and add lemon juice to taste. Serve over hot pasta cooked al dente and garnish with the chopped dill.

Serves 4

Green Mango and Lobster Curry

INGREDIENTS

370mL/13fl oz coconut cream
1 teaspoon Thai green curry paste
1 stalk fresh lemon grass, bruised
    or $1/2$ teaspoon dried lemon grass,
    soaked in hot water until soft
4 kaffir lime leaves, finely sliced
1 large green (unripe) mango,
    cut into 5mm/$1/4$in thick slices
510g/18oz lobster meat,
    cut into 5cm/2in cubes
1 tablespoon palm or brown sugar
2 tablespoons Thai fish sauce (nam pla)
1 tablespoon coconut vinegar
55g/2oz fresh coriander (cilantro) leaves

METHOD

1. Place the coconut cream, curry paste, lemon grass and lime leaves in a saucepan and bring to the boil then reduce the heat and simmer for 5 minutes or until fragrant.

2. Add the mango and simmer for 3 minutes. Add the lobster, sugar and fish sauce and simmer for 7–8 minutes or until the lobster is cooked. Stir in the vinegar and coriander (cilantro).

Serves 4

Lobster Lasagne

INGREDIENTS

8 lasagne noodles, cooked and drained
255g/9oz chopped onion
30g/1oz butter
225g/8oz cream cheese, softened
1 egg, beaten
310g/11oz chopped dill pickles
2 teaspoons chopped basil
285mL/10fl oz cans cream of
   mushroom soup
1/2 cup milk
85mL/3fl oz white wine or chicken broth
85mL/3fl oz seafood sauce

310g/11oz can lobster meat, thawed
   and drained (several pieces of lobster
   meat can be set aside for a garnish,
   if desired)
285g/10oz scallops, thawed if frozen
   and cut in half
85g/3oz grated Parmesan cheese
255g/9oz mozzarella cheese

METHOD

1. Arrange 4 noodles to cover the bottom of an oiled 23cm x 33cm/9in x 13in baking dish. Sauté the onion in the butter just until tender. Stir in the cream cheese, egg, pickles and basil, mixing well. Spread half of this cheese mixture over the noodles.

2. Combine the soup, milk, wine, seafood sauce, lobster and scallops and fold over until well mixed. Spread half over the cheese mixture. Repeat layers with the remaining noodles, cheese and seafood mixture. Sprinkle with Parmesan cheese.

3. Bake, uncovered at 180°C/350°F/Gas 4 for 40 minutes or until heated through. Sprinkle with mozzarella cheese and bake for 2–3 minutes longer or until the cheese melts. Remove from the oven and let stand for 15 minutes before serving.

Serves 10–12

Italian Lobster Pie

INGREDIENTS

1 1/2 cups water
1/4 cup long-grain rice
225g/8oz skim milk ricotta cheese
2 each eggs, beaten
225g/8oz mozzarella cheese, chopped
225g/8oz lobster meat, cut in small pieces
1 small onion, chopped
pinch black pepper
2 tablespoons Italian seasoned
   bread crumbs
2 tablespoons milk

METHOD

1. In a large saucepan bring water to a boil. Add rice and return to boiling, then reduce heat. Cover and simmer 20-25 minutes, or until done. Drain.

2. Stir in ricotta cheese, eggs, mozzarella cheese, lobster meat, onion, and black pepper.

3. Butter an 30cm/12in quiche dish, coat with bread crumbs. Spoon lobster mixture into dish. Pour milk over mixture (this makes top brown and crusty after baking). Bake uncovered at 180°C/350°F/Gas 4 for 45-50 minutes or until top is golden brown and knife inserted near centre comes out clean.

Serves 4

Grilled Creamy Lobster

INGREDIENTS

3 medium, cooked lobsters

45g/1¹/₂oz butter or margarine

1 small onion, chopped

3 tablespoons flour

340mL/12fl oz milk

3 tablespoons cherry liqueur

2 tablespoons grated mild
  Cheddar cheese

2 teaspoons French mustard

¹/₂ teaspoon English mustard

breadcrumbs

extra butter

METHOD

1. Halve the lobsters lengthwise and remove the meat. Cut into chunks. Melt the butter and sauté the onions until tender. Add the flour and stir over a low heat for 2 minutes. Gradually add the milk and allow the sauce to thicken.

2. Add the liqueur and simmer for 2 minutes then stir in the cheese and mustards. Spoon a little of the sauce into the lobster shells, add the lobster and coat with the remaining sauce. Sprinkle with breadcrumbs and dot with butter. Grill until brown and bubbling. Serve immediately.

Serves 6

Lobster Fradiavolo

INGREDIENTS

2 x 680g/24oz lobsters

4 tablespoons olive oil

2 teaspoons minced garlic

115g/4oz minced onion

115g/4oz minced celery

115g/4oz minced green capsicum
  (bell pepper)

55g/2oz chopped parsley

¹/₄ teaspoon black pepper

1 dash Tabasco sauce

1 dash Worcestershire sauce

¹/₂ teaspoon oregano

¹/₂ teaspoon basil

2 each medium, skinned, diced tomatoes

¹/₂ cup marsala

55g/2oz cooked pasta

55g/2oz Parmesan cheese

METHOD

1. Prepare the fresh lobster as outlined in page 6, and then cook in boiling water. Remove from the water, lay the lobsters on their backs and cut them in half lengthwise with a chef's knife. Remove the intestinal tract that runs down the back of the tail section and the stomach. Save the tomalley (soft green liver) and the roe in a separate bowl to add later on.

2. In a large skillet, place the olive oil and garlic. Cook on high heat until the garlic starts to brown. Add the onions, celery, capsicum (bell pepper), parsley, black pepper, Tabasco, Worcestershire, oregano and basil.

3. Cook over medium heat for 4–5 minutes then add the lobsters, split-side down. Pour the tomatoes, marsala, tomalley (soft green liver) and roe over the lobsters, cover and cook on medium heat for 8–10 minutes. In a large shallow bowl, place 225g/8oz of the pasta. Remove the lobsters from the pan and place, the split-side up, on the pasta. Cover with the sauce, sprinkle with Parmesan cheese and serve.

Serves 4

GRILLED CREAMY
LOBSTER

Stuffed Spiny Lobster

INGREDIENTS

1 dried cloud-ear mushroom

2 live 455g/1 lb spiny lobsters

**4 fresh shiitake mushrooms, washed
and stems removed, or 4 fresh brown
mushrooms, washed and trimmed**

1/4 medium carrot

2 stalks green asparagus, trimmed

7 tablespoons bonito stock (dashi)

1 tablespoon light soy sauce

1 tablespoon mirin

3 eggs, lightly beaten

METHOD

1. Soak the cloud-ear mushrooms for 1 hour. Cut the lobster in half lengthwise and remove the meat, reserving the shells. Cut the meat into 8 equal portions and drop in boiling water. When the surface of the meat whitens, immediately drain and plunge into iced water. Drain again and wipe dry.

2. Wash the shells thoroughly and boil in lightly salted water until they turn red.

3. Cut the shiitake (or brown) mushrooms into thin strips. Cut the cloud-ear mushrooms, carrot, and asparagus into 4cm/1$1/2$ in long slivers.

4. Preheat the oven to 220°C/440°F/Gas 7.

5. Combine the bonito stock and all the vegetables in a soup pot and bring to the boil over high heat. Season with soy sauce and mirin and boil for about 3 minutes until the vegetables are just tender. Pour in the beaten egg in a circular motion to cover, and stir gently.

6. Cover with a plate, which fits down inside the pan and sits directly onto the food, and turn off the heat (this ensures even heat and flavour distribution by forcing the rising heat down). Let stand for 2–3 minutes and then drain.

7. Return the lobster to the shells. Top with the egg mixture and place in the preheated oven. When the surface of the egg mixture is lightly browned, remove the lobster from the oven, transfer to plates, and serve.

Serves 4

Lobster à L'Américane

INGREDIENTS

1 lobster, about 1kg/2^1/$_4$ oz

2 tablespoons olive oil

125g/4^1/$_2$oz butter

100mL/3^1/$_2$fl oz brandy

6 shallots

200mL/7fl oz dry white wine

200mL/7fl oz fumet (fish stock)

4 fresh or canned tomatoes

1 sprig tarragon

1 tablespoon finely chopped parsley

salt and pepper

METHOD

1. Buy a live lobster if possible and prepare it as outlined in page 6. Chop into fairly large pieces, shell and all, collecting and reserving the juices. Discard the sand sac and remove the alimentary tract; reserve the greenish tomalley (soft green liver) and coral, if any.

2. Fry the lobster pieces briskly in olive oil, stirring in 30g/1oz butter until their shell has turned bright orange-red. Drain off excess butter and pour in the brandy. Heat and flame.

3. Peel and finely chop the shallots and sweat in 40g/1^1/$_2$oz of butter in a wide, fairly deep pan. Add the white wine and continue cooking until the wire has evaporated.

4. Add the lobster pieces, their reserved juice and the hot fish stock. Add the blanched, peeled, seeded and chopped tomatoes and the sprig of tarragon. Simmer for 15 minutes. Work the coral into 55g/2oz of butter softened at room temperature. Remove the lobster pieces with a slotted spoon or ladle and place in a heated serving dish. Discard the tarragon.

5. Add the coral butter to the sauce in the pan, stir gently as the butter melts, and add the chopped parsley. Season to taste with salt and freshly ground pepper, pour over the lobster and serve at once.

Serves 4

Lobster Thermidore

INGREDIENTS

4 raw lobster tails

15g/^{1}/$_2$oz butter

1^1/$_2$ tablespoons plain flour

1 cup milk

2 teaspoons German mustard

1 teaspoon wholegrain mustard

55mL/3fl oz cream

Crunchy Topping

2 tablespoon Parmesan cheese, grated 2

85g/3oz dry breadcrumbs

1 tablespoon chopped chives

^{1}/$_2$ teaspoon lemon rind, grated

15mL/^{1}/$_2$fl oz butter, melted

METHOD

1. Remove the flesh from the tails and chop into bite-sized pieces. Add the lobster shells to a large saucepan of boiling water, and cook for 1 minute (or until the shells change colour). Drain shells, rinse under cold water and dry.

2. Melt the butter in saucepan, stir in the flour and stir over moderate heat for about 1 minute. Remove from the heat and gradually add the milk, stirring constantly. Cook until the mixture boils and thickens.

3. Stir in the mustards and lobster flesh and cook over medium heat for about 2 minutes, or until lobster is cooked.

4. Remove from the heat, and stir in the cream. Spoon mixture into the lobster shells.

9. Mix all the topping ingredients in a bowl then sprinkle over the prepared lobster mixture. Place under griller for 5–8 minutes, until golden brown).

Serves 4

Lobster in Mint Pesto

INGREDIENTS

**2 uncooked lobster tails,
  halved lengthwise**

Mint Pesto
**1 bunch fresh mint
4 tablespoons almonds, toasted
1 clove garlic, crushed
55mL/2fl oz lime juice
55mL/2fl oz olive oil**

METHOD

1. To make the pesto, place the mint leaves, almonds, garlic and lime juice in a food processor or blender and process to finely chop. With the machine running, slowly add the oil and make a smooth paste.

2. Preheat the oven temperature 200°C/400°F and place the lobster on a baking tray, spread the flesh with pesto and bake for 15–20 minutes or until the lobster is cooked.

Serves 4

Note: This dish is perfect for a special occasion meal. Start with an antipasto platter – purchase the ingredients from the delicatessen section of your supermarket. Accompany the lobster with boiled new potatoes tossed with olive oil and black pepper and a salad of assorted lettuces and chopped fresh herbs. Finish the meal with a good quality purchased ice cream topped with a tablespoon of your favourite liqueur.

Liz's Lobster

INGREDIENTS

4 small lobster tails
2 cups white wine
85g/3oz butter
2 tablespoons flour
$^1/_2$ cup cream
1 teaspoon lemon juice
$^1/_2$ teaspoon Dijon mustard
1 tablespoon capers, chopped
cooked rice to serve

METHOD

1. Simmer the lobster tails in the white wine until tender. Remove the lobster from the wine and set aside. Reduce the wine to $^1/_2$ cup.

2. Melt the butter in a saucepan, add the flour and cook for 1 minute. Gradually add the reduced wine and stir until the sauce has thickened. Add all the remaining ingredients, except the rice, and stir until the sauce is simmering. Remove from the heat.

3. To serve, place the lobster tails on top of a bed of rice and top with the sauce. Garnish with fresh steamed asparagus.

Serves 2

Lobster Quiche

INGREDIENTS

6 each well beaten eggs

680mL/24fl oz sour cream

1/2 teaspoon Worcestershire sauce

1/4 teaspoon black pepper

1 teaspoon Dijon mustard

1 pie shell (see savoury tart pastry)

255g/9oz grated Swiss cheese

255g/9oz grated sharp Cheddar cheese

1/2 tablespoon chopped
   spring onions (scallions)

170g/6oz chopped lobster meat

paprika, for sprinkling

METHOD

1. Preheat the oven to 190°C/375°F/Gas 5. In a medium-sized mixing bowl, blend the eggs, sour cream, Worcestershire, pepper and Dijon mustard together. (This is the quiche batter) Arrange pie dough in a pie shell. In a seperate bowl, toss the two cheeses with the spring onions (scallions) and lobster. Place the lobster mixture into the pie shell. Add the quiche batter, sprinkle with paprika and bake until set and a knife inserted near centre comes out clean (about 25–35 minutes. Let cool; serve at room temperature.

Serves 4

Chinese Lobster Stir-fry

INGREDIENTS

510g/18oz lobster meat, fresh or frozen

2 tablespoons oil

1 small clove garlic, minced

1/2 cup chicken broth

1 small red capsicum (bell pepper)

255g/9oz bean sprouts

255g/9oz water chestnuts

255g/9oz broccoli

370g/13oz Chinese cabbage, chopped

1/2 teaspoon salt

1/4 teaspoon pepper

1 egg, lightly beaten

METHOD

1. If frozen, thaw and chop the lobster into bite size pieces. In a skillet sauté the lobster and garlic in the oil for 1 minute. Add the broth and vegetables and simmer, uncovered, for 5 minutes. Season with salt and pepper.

2. Add a little of the hot broth to the beaten egg. Stir the egg mixture into the vegetables and lobster. Heat gently but do not boil. Serve with rice.

Serves 4

Savoury Tart Pastry

INGREDIENTS

2 cups flour

1/2 teaspoon salt

1/4 cup cold un-salted butter

2 egg yolks

4–6 tablespoons ice water

METHOD

1. sift flour and salt together onto work surface; make a well in the centre.

2 Place butter, yolks and 3 tablespoons of the water in the well. Using fingertips, pinch butter to mix with the waterand yolks. With a dough scraper or pastry blender, gradually work flour into yolk mixture with a cutting motion to make coarse crumbs.

3. Gather crumbs into a rough mound. Work small portions of the dough against the work surface with the heel of your hand (pushing away from you), so that the dough is smeared across the work areasurface (this is known as fraisage; it distributes the ingredients evenly through the dough. 4. When pieces of dough are pliable and peel away from the surface in one piece, press into a ball. Wrap well and refrigerate until firm (about 2 hours)

4. Roll out pastry and use to line a tart tin that has a removable bottom. Blind bake until fully baked; cool.

Makes enough dough for one 25 x 5cm/10 x 2in tart tin.

CHINESE LOBSTER STIR-FRY

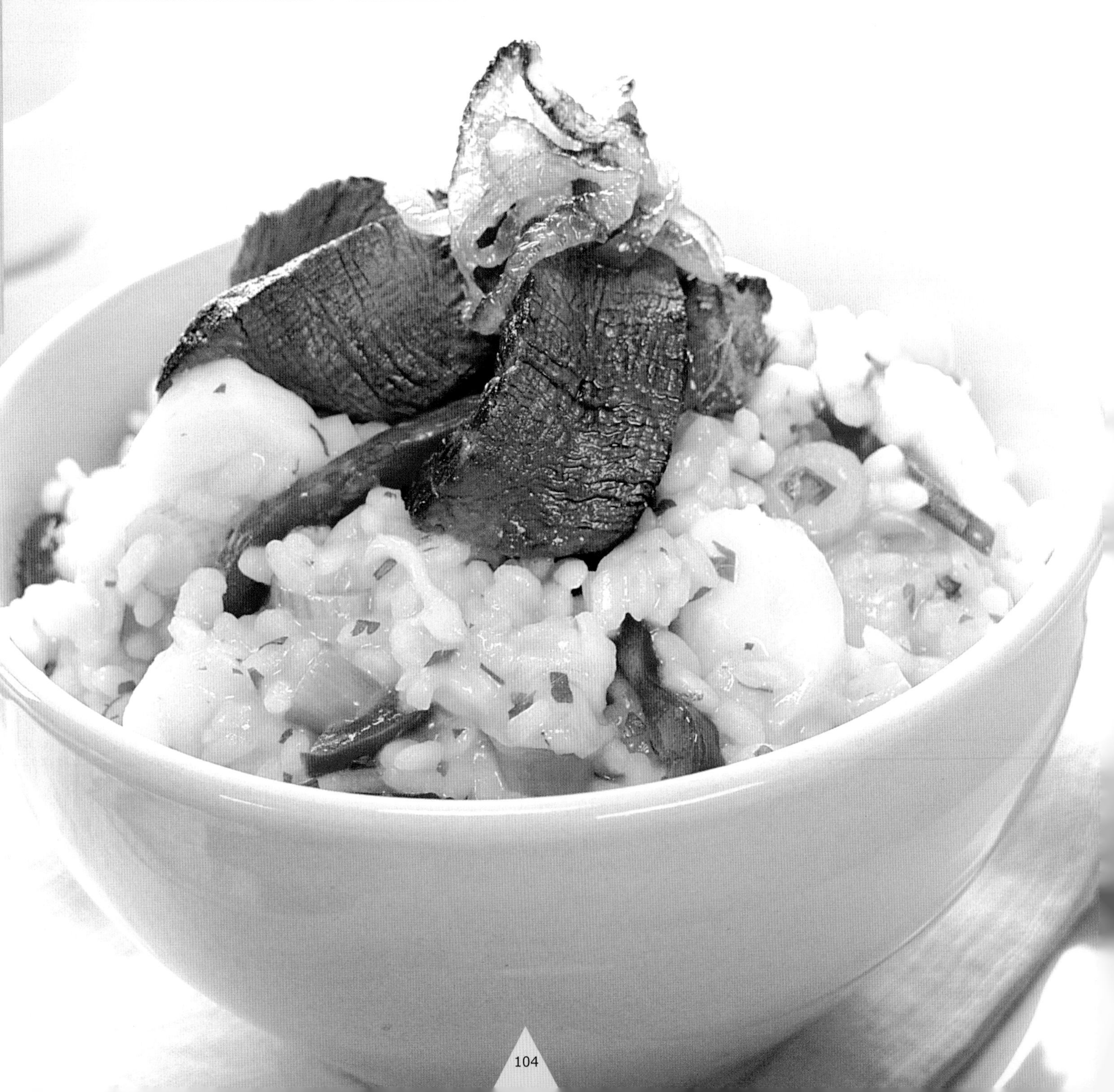

Surf and Turf Risotto

INGREDIENTS

2 tablespoons olive oil

4 cloves garlic

400g/14oz eye fillet, cut into 2 pieces

10 spring onions (scallions), chopped

1 red capsicum (bell pepper), sliced
   into strips

400g/14oz arborio rice

$1/2$ cup white wine

4 cups rich vegetable or
   chicken stock, simmering

2 lobster tails, cooked

2 onions, peeled and sliced

oil, for frying

1 tablespoon Parmesan cheese, grated

lots of fresh parsley, chopped

1 tablespoon sour cream

METHOD

1. Heat the olive oil and gently fry the garlic for a moment or two. Add the beef and sauté until seared and crisp on both sides. Remove from the pan and keep warm, wrapped in foil (For medium or well-done beef, bake at 200°C/400°F/Gas 6 for 5 minutes or 10 minutes respectively, then keep warm wrapped in foil.)

2. To the oil and garlic mixture, add the spring onions (scallions) and capsicum (bell pepper) strips and sauté until softened.

3. Add the rice and stir to coat, then add the wine and simmer to evaporate the alcohol while the liquid is absorbed. When the rice mixture is firm, add the stock, half a cup at a time, stirring well after each addition and allowing each quantity of stock to be absorbed before the next addition. Continue in this fashion until the stock has all been incorporated. With the last addition of stock, add the lobster meat, cut into attractive, manageable pieces, and stir to distribute.

4. Peel and slice the onions. Either deep-fry at 180°C/350°F until crisp and golden, or alternatively, toss with 2 tablespoons of olive oil and bake at 220°C/425°F for 30–40 minutes, tossing frequently, until golden. Set aside until the risotto is finished and ready to serve.

5. When almost all of the liquid has been absorbed and the rice is 'al dente', stir through the Parmesan cheese, parsley and sour cream.

6. Meanwhile, remove the warm meat from the foil and slice thinly. Serve the risotto in individual bowls, fan out the meat and place on top of the risotto. Garnish with the crispy fried (or baked) onions and serve immediately.

Serves 4

King Island Lobster, Summer Herbs and Crustacean-infused Olive Oil

INGREDIENTS

400g/14oz lobster

court bouillon (see recipe on page 75)

salt and pepper

20mL/²/₃oz olive oil

2 small potatoes, cooked and peeled

pinch of chervil, chives and tarragon

2 tomatoes

¹/₄ avocado

¹/₂ piece green mango

6 slices cucumber, skin removed

30g/1oz mixed seasonal lettuce

55mL/2fl oz crustacean oil

6 lobster tuilles

Lobster Tuilles

1 cup lobster stock

30g/1oz flour

20g/²/₃oz butter

1 egg white

dash of lemon juice

sesame seeds

METHOD

1. Immerse the lobster in boiling court bouillon for approximately 6 minutes. Drain and allow to cool, keeping the lobster ³/₄ cooked.

2. Remove the meat from the shell keeping the tail intact; extract all the meat from the joints and legs. Slice the lobster tail into medallions and season with salt and pepper and a little olive oil. Finely dice the meat from the legs along with the end pieces of the tail. Lightly grill the lobster medallions. Slice the cooked potatoes, whilst still warm, into small rounds. Pinch the chervil and tarragon, chop the chives. Blanch, peel and de-seed tomatoes, reserve enough for the 2 tomato rounds and dice the remaining along with the avocado. Add this to the chopped chives and chopped lobster and season.

3. Mound the mixture into the middle of the plate; garnish with strips of green mango, tomato and cucumber. Top with the grilled lobster medallions and potatoes. Dress the lettuce and place on top of the avocado mixture; sprinkle with the chervil and tarragon.

4. Drizzle the lobster slices with crustacean oil, garnish with lobster tuilles and serve.

5. To make the lobster tuille reduce the lobster stock to a syrupy consistency – approximately ¹/₃ cup. Combine the flour and butter to form a paste. Mix in the reduction, salt, pepper, lemon juice and the egg white, a little at a time. Spread onto a greased tray as a sheet or pass through a stencil. Sprinkle with sesame seeds and bake at 180°C/350°F/Gas 4 until golden brown (approximately 10 minutes).

Serves 4

SEAFOOD PIZZA

Seafood Pizza

INGREDIENTS

ready-to-use pizza bases

pasta sauce

mushrooms

chopped mixed vegetables, to taste

grated cheese (combine Mozzarella,
   Cheddar and Monteray Jack)

variety of cooked seafood such as mussels,
   lobster meat, crab meat, flaked fish,
   clams

METHOD

1. Allow everyone to assemble their own pizzas.

2. Spread the crust with tomato sauce, add vegetables and seafood and top with cheese.

3. Be sure to have everyone place something different on the top of their own pizza so that you know whose is whose when it comes to the eating.

4. Place on the top rack of aa oven to 200°C/400°F/Gas 6, until the cheese melts and the pizzas are heated through.

Serves a tribe

Crab-stuffed Pasta Shells

INGREDIENTS

680g/24oz crab meat

680g/24oz cream cheese

170g/6oz grated Parmesan cheese

1 teaspoon minced garlic

55g/2oz chopped shallots

fresh ground pepper, to taste

85g/3oz chopped fresh tarragon
   or 1 tablespoon dried

1/2 teaspoon red capsicum (bell pepper)
   flakes

225g/8oz large pasta shells

2 tomatoes, peeled, seeded, and chopped

grated Parmesan cheese to garnish

4 cups double cream

2 teaspoons minced garlic

2 tablespoons chopped shallots

salt and pepper, to taste

METHOD

1. Blend the first 8 ingredients and adjust the seasonings. Cook the pasta shells according to the instructions on the package. Prepare the cream sauce by combining the last 4 ingredients in a saucepan and heating until the mixture is reduced by half.

2. Pour the reduced cream sauce into a shallow baking dish that will hold the shells in one layer. Stuff the shells with the crab meat mixture, arrange them on top of the sauce, and bake, covered, at 200°C/400°F/Gas 6, for 15–20 minutes. Remove from the oven and top with the chopped tomato and Parmesan cheese.

Serves 8–10

Lobster Cheese Casserole

INGREDIENTS

510g/18oz lobster meat, diced

2 tablespoons butter

50g/1¾oz flour

170mL/6fl oz milk

310mL/11fl oz whipping cream

125g/4½oz Cheddar cheese, grated

½ teaspoon salt

170g/6oz green capsicum
   (bell pepper), diced

55g/2oz Cheddar cheese, extra grated

pinch of paprika

METHOD

1. Place the lobster in a greased 1 L/35oz casserole dish. Over low heat, melt the butter, blend in the flour and slowly add the milk and cream. Cook, stirring constantly until the mixture is thick and smooth. Add the 125g/4½ oz cheese and the salt and green capsicum (bell pepper). Stir until cheese the melts. Pour over the lobster. Sprinkle 55g/2oz cheese over top and garnish with paprika.

2. Bake at 180°C/350°F/Gas 4 for 15 minutes. Grill for 2 minutes to brown the top.

Serves 4–6

Crab Supreme

INGREDIENTS

225g/8oz butter

1 onion, chopped

1 green capsicum (bell pepper), chopped

225g/8oz flour

2 teaspoons dry mustard

½ teaspoon salt

2 cups milk

510g/18oz grated Cheddar cheese

2 teaspoons Worcestershire sauce

800g/28oz can tomatoes,
   drained and chopped

455g/16oz crab meat (fresh or canned)

METHOD

1. Melt the butter in a large saucepan. Sauté the onion and capsicum (bell pepper) in the butter until softened. Combine the flour, mustard and salt. Remove the pan from the heat and whisk in the flour mixture until smooth. Add the milk, stirring constantly and return to the heat. Add cheese to pan. Cook, stirring constantly, on medium until the cheese has melted and the sauce is smooth and thick. Stir in the Worcestershire sauce. Add the tomatoes and crab meat.

2. Pour into a casserole dish and bake at 200°C/400°F/Gas 6 for 20 minutes until hot and bubbly. Serve over rice.

Serves 6

LOBSTER CHEESE CASSEROLE

Lobster Mornay

INGREDIENTS
1 medium lobster cooked and halved

Mornay Sauce
310mL/11fl oz milk
1 bay leaf
1 small onion, chopped
5 black peppercorns
30g/1oz butter
2 tablespoons plain flour
65mL/2¼fl oz cream
65g/2¼oz cheese, grated
salt and cracked black peppercorns
15mL/½fl oz butter, extra, melted
65g/2¼oz fresh breadcrumbs

METHOD
1. Remove the lobster meat from the shells and cut into bite-sized pieces. Reserve the shells.

2. In a saucepan, place the milk, bay leaf, onion and peppercorns. Heat slowly to boiling point. Remove from the heat, cover and stand for 10 minutes. Strain.

3. In a pan, heat the butter, then remove from the heat. Stir in the flour and blend, gradually adding the strained milk. Return the pan to the heat, and stir constantly until the sauce boils and thickens. Simmer the sauce for 1 minute. Remove from the heat, add the cream, cheese, salt and pepper. Stir the sauce until the cheese melts, and add the lobster.

4. Divide the mixture between the shells. Melt extra butter in a small pan, add the breadcrumbs, and stir to combine.

5. Scatter the crumbs over the lobster and brown under a hot grill.

Serves 2

Lobster Creole

INGREDIENTS
30mL/1fl oz olive oil
½ slice medium red onion
½ slice medium green capsicum (bell pepper)
½ slice medium red capsicum (bell pepper)
½ slice medium tomato
½ teaspoon lobster base or fish stock powder
½ cup water
170g/6oz lobster tail and claw meat
½ teaspoon chopped garlic
15mL/½ fl oz red hot sauce
1 teaspoon Cajun seasoning
2 tablespoons non-fat sour cream

METHOD
1. Heat the oil in a sauté pan to medium heat. Add the onion, capsicum (bell peppers), tomato and sauté for 5 minutes. Add the lobster base or stock powder to water until dissolved. Transfer to the sauté pan. Add the lobster meat, garlic, red hot sauce and Cajun seasoning and simmer for 3 more minutes. Stir in the sour cream until desired consistency. Serve over white rice.

Serves 1

LOBSTER MORNAY

Lobster Newburg

INGREDIENTS

55g/2oz butter

**2kg/4¹/₂lb lobster, boiled, shelled
  and cut into small pieces**

2 teaspoons salt

¹/₄ teaspoon ground cayenne pepper

¹/₄ teaspoon ground nutmeg

1 cup double cream

4 egg yolks

2 tablespoons brandy

2 tablespoons dry sherry

**reserved lobster-tail shell or
  4–6 vol-au-vent cases**

rice, for serving

METHOD

1. In a shallow frying pan melt the butter over a moderate heat. When the foam subsides, add the lobster.

2. Cook slowly for about 5 minutes. Add the salt, cayenne pepper and nutmeg.

3. In a small bowl lightly beat the cream with the egg yolks. Add the mixture to the pan, stirring continuously.

4. Finally, add the brandy and sherry as the mass begins to thicken. Do not allow to boil or the sauce will curdle.

5. Serve either placed back in the lobster tail shell or in vol-au-vent cases. Serve with steamed rice.

Serves 4–6

GRILLED LOBSTER AND LEMON ANNISETTE BUTTER

Grilled Lobster and Lemon Annisette Butter

INGREDIENTS

145g/5oz butter

juice 1 lemon

2 tablespoons Pernod

1 teaspoon dill or fennel seeds

3 large green lobster tails

METHOD

1. Melt the butter in a saucepan and add the lemon juice, Pernod and dill. Stir well over medium heat and set to one side. Cut the lobster tails in half, remove the meat and cut into chunks then return the meat to the shell. Sit the tails on a grilling rack, brush liberally with the butter and place under the griller. Grill, brushing regularly with the butter until cooked. Serve with a tossed mixed lettuce and watercress salad.

Serves 6

Louisiana Stuffed Crabs

INGREDIENTS

125g/4^1/2oz margarine

1 onion, finely chopped

1 rib celery, chopped

^{1}/2 capsicum (bell pepper), chopped

485g/17oz crab meat

3 tablespoons minced green onion,
   bulbs only

2 tablespoons minced parsley

salt and pepper, to taste

2 teaspoons lemon juice

1 teaspoon Worcestershire sauce

^{1}/2 teaspoon Tabasco sauce

1 egg beaten with 55mL/2fl oz milk

370g/13oz plain breadcrumbs

buttered breadcrumbs

METHOD

1. Preheat the oven to 200°C/400°F/Gas 6. Melt the margarine in skillet over low heat. Add the onions, celery and capsicum (bell pepper) and cook slowly until tender. Add the crab meat, green onions, and parsley and simmer for about 10 minutes. Add the salt, pepper, lemon juice, Worcestershire sauce, Tabasco and egg-milk mixture. Set aside to cool slightly. Add the plain breadcrumbs to obtain stuffing consistency. Stuff the crab shells and top with the buttered breadcrumbs. Bake for 15 minutes, or until lightly browned.

Serves 8

LOBSTER PROVENÇALE

Lobster Provençale

INGREDIENTS

55g/2oz butter

1 teaspoon freshly crushed garlic

2 spring onions (scallions), chopped

310g/11oz can tomatoes

salt and cracked black peppercorns
   (to taste)

pinch of saffron

1 large cooked lobster

55mL/2fl oz brandy

boiled rice

1/2 bunch fresh chives, chopped,
   for garnish

lemon wedges, for garnish

METHOD

1. In a shallow frying pan, melt the butter over a moderate heat. Add the garlic, spring onions (scallions), tomatoes, salt and pepper, and saffron. Cook until the onions are translucent (about 2 minutes).

2. Remove the meat from the lobster, and cut into large pieces. Add the lobster to the frying pan and flame with the brandy. Cook gently until the lobster is heated through.

3. Place the rice on a serving plate and sprinkle with chives.

4. Remove the lobster from the frying pan, retaining the cooking liquid as a sauce.

5. Arrange the lobster on the rice and spoon the sauce (which has been cooked with the lobster) over the lobster. Serve with the lemon wedges on the side of the plate.

Serves 4

Lobster Forestiere

INGREDIENTS

2 x 485g/17oz fresh lobsters

200mL/7oz light cream

4 tablespoons butter

55g/2oz finely chopped shallots

225g/8oz chopped mushrooms

1 tablespoon flour

2 teaspoons Dijon mustard

1 teaspoon Worcestershire sauce

2 each egg yolks

Tabasco sauce, salt and pepper, to taste

225g/8oz buttered breadcrumbs

2 tablespoons finely chopped parsley

METHOD

1. Steam the lobster in 2cm/^{3}/$_4$in of water for 10 minutes. Strain and reserve 55mL/2fl oz of liquid.

2. Warm the cream in a small saucepan. Melt the butter in another saucepan and sauté the shallots and mushrooms until tender. Stir in the flour and cook until bubbling. Remove from the heat and whisk in the warm cream. Return to the heat and boil, stirring constantly, until the sauce thickens. Simmer for at least 3 minutes. Add the mustard and Worcestershire sauce.

3. Whisk the egg yolks and lobster liquid in a bowl. Whisk in 125mL/4^1/$_2$fl oz of the hot sauce, a spoonful at a time. Slowly beat in the remaining sauce. Add the Tabasco and season to taste. Transfer the enriched sauce to the saucepan and, stirring carefully, bring to a simmer over moderate heat.

4. Arrange the lobsters in their shells on a baking sheet. Distribute the creamed mushroom sauce over the lobsters. Top with a mixture of buttered crumbs and parsley. Bake at 230°C/450°F/Gas 8 for at least 5 minutes until the breadcrumbs begin to brown.

Serves 4

Crab Tempura

INGREDIENTS

6 large crab legs

plain flour

200mL/7fl oz tempura batter (see below)

1 sheet nori seaweed, cut into
  5cm/2in strips

lemon wedges

METHOD

1. Carefully break the shell away from the thick end of each crab leg. Leave the thin end of the leg still covered with shell.

2. Make the tempura batter as described below. Dust the crab meat lightly with flour. Dip the meat end of the crab stick into the tempura batter. Deep-fry the whole leg at 180°C/350°F/Gas 4 until the batter is crisp and golden.

3. Gently tie each of the seaweed strips into a knot, dip into the tempura batter and deep-fry until crispy.

4. Arrange the crab on a large serving plate and garnish with lemon wedges and fried seaweed.

Tempura Batter

Place 1 egg yolk and 1 cup of iced water into a bowl and mix together. Add $1^1/2$ cups of plain flour or tempura flour and mix roughly with chopsticks or a fork. Do not over-mix, the mixture should be lumpy. Use immediately while batter is still cold.

Serves 3

WEIGHTS & MEASURES

ooking is not an exact science: one does not require finely calibrated scales, pipettes and scientific equipment to cook, yet the conversion to metric measures in some countries and its interpretations must have intimidated many a good cook.

Weights are given in the recipes only for ingredients such as meats, fish, poultry and some vegetables. Though a few grams/ounces one way or another will not affect the success of your dish.

Though recipes have been tested using the Australian Standard 250mL cup, 20mL tablespoon and 5mL teaspoon, they will work just as well with the US and Canadian 8fl oz cup, or the UK 300mL cup. We have used graduated cup measures in preference to tablespoon measures so that proportions are always the same. Where tablespoon measures have been given, these are not crucial measures, so using the smaller tablespoon of the US or UK will not affect the recipe's success. At least we all agree on the teaspoon size.

For breads, cakes and pastries, the only area which might cause concern is where eggs are used, as proportions will then vary. If working with a 250mL or 300mL cup, use large eggs (60g/2oz), adding a little more liquid to the recipe for 300mL cup measures if it seems necessary. Use the medium-sized eggs (55g/1$1/2$oz) with 8fl oz cup measure. A graduated set of measuring cups and spoons is recommended, the cups in particular for measuring dry ingredients. Remember to level such ingredients to ensure their accuracy.

English Measures

All measurements are similar to Australian with two exceptions: the English cup measures 300mL/10fl oz, whereas the Australian cup measure 250mL/8fl oz. The English tablespoon (the Australian dessertspoon) measures 14.8mL/$1/2$fl oz against the Australian tablespoon of 20mL/3/4fl oz.

American Measures

The American reputed pint is 16fl oz, a quart is equal to 32fl oz and the American gallon, 128fl oz. The Imperial measurement is 20fl oz to the pint, 40fl oz a quart and 160fl oz one gallon. The American tablespoon is equal to 14.8mL/$1/2$ fl oz, the teaspoon is 5mL/$1/6$ fl oz. The cup measure is 250mL/8fl oz, the same as Australia.

Dry Measures

All the measures are level, so when you have filled a cup or spoon, level it off with the edge of a knife. The scale below is the 'cook's equivalent'; it is not an exact conversion of metric to imperial measurement. To calculate the exact metric equivalent yourself, use 2.2046lb = 1kg or 1lb = 0.45359kg

Metric	Imperial
g = grams	oz = ounces
kg = kilograms	lb = pound
15g	$1/2$oz
20g	$2/3$oz
30g	1oz
55g	2oz
85g	3oz
115g	4oz/$1/4$ lb
145g	5oz
170g	6oz
200g	7oz
225g	8oz/$1/2$ lb
255g	9oz
285g	10oz
310g	11oz
340g	12oz/$3/4$ lb
370g	13oz
400g	14oz
425g	15oz
1,000g	1kg/ 35.2oz/2.2
1.5kg	3.3 lb

WEIGHTS & MEASURES

Oven Temperatures

The Celsius temperatures given here are not exact; they have been rounded off and are given as a guide only. Follow the manufacturer's temperature guide, relating it to oven description given in the recipe. Remember gas ovens are hottest at the top, electric ovens at the bottom and convection-fan forced ovens are usually even throughout. We included Regulo numbers for gas cookers which may assist.

To convert °C to °F multiply °C by 9 and divide by 5 then add 32.

Oven temperatures

	C°	F°	Regular
Very slow	120	250	1
Slow	150	300	2
Moderately slow	160	325	3
Moderate	180	350	4
Moderately hot	190–200	370–400	5–6
Hot	210–220	410–440	6–7
Very hot	230	450	8
Super hot	250–290	475–500	9–10

Cake dish sizes

Metric	Imperial
15cm	6in
18cm	7in
20cm	8in
23cm	9in

Loaf dish sizes

Metric	Imperial
23x12cm	9x5in
25x8cm	10x3in
28x18cm	11x7in

Liquid Measurements

The scale following is the 'cook's equivalent'; it is not an exact conversion of metric to imperial measurement. To calculate the exact equivalent yourself, divide millilitres by 28.349523 to obtain fluid ounce equivelant, or multiply fluid ounces by 28.349523 to obtain millilitre equivalant.

Liquid measures

Metric millilitres mL	Imperial fl oz	Cup & Spoon fluid ounce
5mL	$1/6$ fl oz	1 teaspoon
20mL	$2/3$ fl oz	1 tablespoon
30mL	1fl oz	(1 tablespoon plus 2 teaspoons)
60mL	2fl oz	$1/4$ cup
100mL	3fl oz	$1/3$ cup
125mL	4fl oz	$1/2$ cup
150mL	5fl oz	
250mL	8fl oz	1 cup
300mL	10fl oz	
380mL	12fl oz	$1^1/2$ cups
400mL	14fl oz	$1^3/4$ cups
500mL	16fl oz	2 cups
600mL	20fl oz	$2^1/2$ cups
1 litre	36fl oz	4 cups

Cup measurements

One cup is equal to the following weights.

	Metric	Imperial
Almonds, flaked	90g	3oz
Almonds, slivered, ground	115g	4oz
Almonds, kernel	145g	5oz
Apples, dried, chopped	115g	4oz
Apricots, dried, chopped	170g	6oz
Breadcrumbs, packet	115g	4oz
Breadcrumbs, soft	55g	2oz
Cheese, grated	115g	4oz
Choc bits	145g	5oz
Coconut, desiccated	85g	3oz
Cornflakes	30g	1oz
Currants	145g	5oz
Flour	115g	4oz
Fruit, dried (mixed, sultanas etc)	170g	6oz
Ginger, crystallised, glace	225g	8oz
Honey, treacle, golden syrup	285g	10oz
Mixed peel	200g	7oz
Nuts, chopped	115g	4oz
Prunes, chopped	200g	7oz
Rice, cooked	145g	5oz
Rice, uncooked	200g	7oz
Rolled oats	85g	3oz
Sesame seeds	115g	4oz
Shortening (butter, margarine)	225g	8oz
Sugar, brown	145g	5oz
Sugar, granulated or caster	225g	8oz
Sugar, sifted icing	145g	5oz
Wheatgerm	55g	2oz

Length

Some of us still have trouble converting imperial length to metric. In this scale, measures have been rounded off to the easiest-to-use and most acceptable figures.
To obtain the exact metric equivalent in converting inches to centimetres, multiply inches by 2.54 whereby 1 inch equals 25.4 millimetres and 1 millimetre equals 0.03937 inches.

Metric mm = millimetres cm = centimetres	Imperial in = inches ft = feet
5mm, 0.5cm	$1/4$ in
10mm, 1.0cm	$1/2$ in
20mm, 2.0cm	$3/4$ in
$2^1/2$cm	1in
5cm	2in
$7^1/2$cm	3in
10cm	4in
$12^1/2$cm	5in
15cm	6in
18cm	7in
20cm	8in
23cm	9in
25cm	10in
28cm	11in
30cm	1ft, 12in

GLOSSARY

acidulated water: water with added acid, such as lemon juice or vinegar, which prevents discoloration of ingredients, particularly fruit or vegetables. The proportion of acid to water is 1 teaspoon per 300mL.

al dente: Italian cooking term for ingredients that are cooked until tender but still firm to the bite; usually applied to pasta.

americaine: method of serving seafood - usually lobster and monkfish - in a sauce flavoured with olive oil, aromatic herbs, tomatoes, white wine, fish stock, brandy and tarragon.

anglaise: cooking style for simple cooked dishes such as boiled vegetables. Assiette anglaise is a plate of cold cooked meats.

antipasto: Italian for "before the meal", it denotes an assortment of cold meats, vegetables and cheeses, often marinated, served as an hors d'oeuvre. A typical antipasto might include salami, prosciutto, marinated artichoke hearts, anchovy fillets, olives, tuna fish and Provolone cheese.

au gratin: food sprinkled with breadcrumbs, often covered with cheese sauce and browned until a crisp coating forms.

balsamic vinegar: a mild, extremely fragrant wine-based vinegar made in northern Italy. Traditionally, the vinegar is aged for at least seven years in a series of casks made of various woods.

baste: to moisten food while it is cooking by spooning or brushing on liquid or fat.

baine marie: a saucepan standing in a large pan which is filled with boiling water to keep liquids at simmering point. A double boiler will do the same job.

beat: to stir thoroughly and vigorously.

beurre manie: equal quantities of butter and flour kneaded together and added a little at a time to thicken a stew or casserole.

bird: see paupiette.

blanc: a cooking liquid made by adding flour and lemon juice to water in order to keep certain vegetables from discolouring as they cook.

blanch: to plunge into boiling water and then in some cases, into cold water. Fruits and nuts are blanched to remove skin easily.

blanquette: a white stew of lamb, veal or chicken, bound with egg yolks and cream and accompanied by onion and mushrooms.

blend: to mix thoroughly.

bonne femme: dishes cooked in the traditional French "housewife" style. Chicken and pork bonne femme are garnished with bacon, potatoes and baby onion; fish bonne femme with mushrooms in a white wine sauce.

bouquet garni: a bunch of herbs, usually consisting of sprigs of parsley, thyme, marjoram, rosemary, a bay leaf, peppercorns and cloves, tied in muslin and used to flavour stews and casseroles.

braise: to cook whole or large pieces of poultry, game, fish, meat or vegetables in a small amount of wine, stock or other liquid in a closed pot. Often the main ingredient is first browned in fat and then cooked in a low oven or very slowly on top of the stove. Braising suits tough meats and older birds and produces a mellow, rich sauce.

broil: the American term for grilling food.

brown: cook in a small amount of fat until brown.

burghul (also bulgur): a type of cracked wheat, where the kernels are steamed and dried before being crushed.

buttered: to spread with softened or melted butter.

butterfly: to slit a piece of food in half horizontally, cutting it almost through so that when opened it resembles butterfly wings. Chops, large prawns and thick fish fillets are often butterflied so that they cook more quickly.

buttermilk: a tangy, low-fat cultured milk product whose slight acidity makes it an ideal marinade base for poultry.

calzone: a semicircular pocket of pizza dough, stuffed with meat or vegetables, sealed and baked.

caramelise: to melt sugar until it is a golden brown syrup.

champignons: small mushrooms, usually canned.

chasseur: (hunter) a French cooking style in which meat and chicken dishes are cooked with mushrooms, shallots, white wine, and often tomato.

clarify: to melt butter and drain the oil off the sediment.

coat: to cover with a thin layer of flour, sugar, nuts, crumbs, poppy or sesame seeds, cinnamon sugar or a few of the ground spices.

concasser: to chop coarsely, usually tomatoes.

confit: from the French verb confire, meaning to preserve. Food that is made into a preserve by cooking very slowly and thoroughly until tender. In the case of meat, such as duck or goose, it is cooked in its own fat, and covered with it so that it does not come into contact with the air. Vegetables such as onions are good inconfit.

consomme: a clear soup usually made from beef.

coulis: a thin puree, usually of fresh or cooked fruit or vegetables, which is soft enough to pour (couler means to run). A coulis may be rough-textured or very smooth.

court bouillon: the liquid in which fish, poultry or meat is cooked. It usually consists of water with bay leaf, onion, carrots and salt and freshly ground black pepper to taste. Other additives can include wine, vinegar, stock, garlic or spring onions (scallions).

couscous: cereal processed from semolina into pellets, traditionally steamed and served with meat and vegetables in the classic North African stew of the same name.

cruciferous vegetables: certain members of the mustard, cabbage and turnip families with cross-shaped flowers and strong aromas and flavours.

cream: to make soft, smooth and creamy by rubbing with back of spoon or by beating with mixer. Usually applied to fat and sugar.

croutons: small toasted or fried cubes of bread.

crudites: raw vegetables, whether cut in slices or sticks to nibble plain or with a dipping sauce, or shredded and tossed as salad with a simple dressing.

cube: to cut into small pieces with 6 equal sides.

curdle: to cause milk or sauce to separate into solid and liquid. Example, overcooked egg mixtures.

daikon radish (also called mooli): a long white Japanese radish.

dark sesame oil (also called Oriental sesame oil): dark polyunsaturated oil with a low burning point, used for seasoning. Do not replace with lighter sesame oil.

deglaze: to dissolve congealed cooking juices or glaze on the bottom of a pan by adding a liquid, then scraping and stirring vigorously whilst bringing the liquid to the boil. Juices may be used to make gravy or to add to sauce.

degrease: to skim grease from the surface of liquid. If possible the liquid should be chilled so the fat solidifies. If not, skim off most of the fat with a large metal spoon, then trail strips of paper towel on the surface of the liquid to remove any remaining globules.

devilled: a dish or sauce that is highly seasoned with a hot ingredient such as mustard, Worcestershire sauce or cayenne pepper.

dice: to cut into small cubes.

dietary fibre: a plant-cell material that is undigested or only partially digested in the human body, but which promotes healthy digestion of other food matter.

dissolve: mix a dry ingredient with liquid until absorbed.

dredge: to coat with a dry ingredient, as flour or sugar.

drizzle: to pour in a fine thread-like stream over a surface.

dust: to sprinkle or coat lightly with flour or icing sugar.

Dutch oven: a heavy casserole with a lid usually made from cast iron or pottery.

emulsion: a mixture of two liquids that are not mutually soluble - for example, oil and water.

entree: in Europe, the "entry" or hors d'oeuvre; in North America entree means the main course.

fillet: special cut of beef, lamb, pork or veal; breast of poultry and game; fish cut off the bone lengthways.

flake: to break into small pieces with a fork.

flame: to ignite warmed alcohol over food.

fold in: a gentle, careful combining of a light or delicate mixture with a heavier mixture using a metal spoon.

fricassee: a dish in which poultry, fish or vegetables are bound together with a white or veloute sauce. In Britain and the United States, the name applies to an old-fashioned dish of chicken in a creamy sauce.

galette: sweet or savoury mixture shaped as a flat round.

garnish: to decorate food, usually with something edible.

gastrique: caramelized sugar deglazed with vinegar and used in fruit-flavoured savoury sauces, in such dishes as duck with orange.

glaze: a thin coating of beaten egg, syrup or aspic which is brushed over pastry, fruits or cooked meats.

gluten: a protein in flour that is developed when dough is kneaded, making it elastic.

gratin: a dish cooked in the oven or under the grill so that it develops a brown crust. Breadcrumbs or cheese may be sprinkled on top first. Shallow gratin dishes ensure a maximum area of crust.

grease: to rub or brush lightly with oil or fat.

infuse: to immerse herbs, spices or other flavourings in hot liquid to flavour it. Infusion takes from two to five minutes depending on the flavouring. The liquid should be very hot but not boiling.

jardiniere: a garnish of garden vegetables, typically carrots, pickling onions, French beans and turnips.

GLOSSARY

joint: to cut poultry, game or small animals into serving pieces by dividing at the joint.

julienne: to cut food into match-like strips.

knead: to work dough using heel of hand with a pressing motion, while stretching and folding the dough.

lights: lungs of an animal, used in various meat preparations such as pates and faggots.

line: to cover the inside of a container with paper, to protect or aid in removing mixture.

macerate: to soak food in liquid to soften.

marinade: a seasoned liquid, usually an oil and acid mixture, in which meats or other foods are soaked to soften and give more flavour.

marinara: Italian "sailor's style" cooking that does not apply to any particular combination of ingredients. Marinara tomato sauce for pasta is most familiar.

marinate: to let food stand in a marinade to season and tenderize.

mask: to cover cooked food with sauce.

melt: to heat until liquified.

mince: to grind into very small pieces.

mix: to combine ingredients by stirring.

monounsaturated fats: one of three types of fats found in foods. Are believed not to raise the level of cholesterol in the blood.

nicoise: a garnish of tomatoes, garlic and black olives; a salad with anchovy, tuna and French beans is typical.

non-reactive pan: a cooking pan whose surface does not chemically react with food. Materials used include stainless steel, enamel, glass and some alloys.

noisette: small "nut" of lamb cut from boned loin or rack that is rolled, tied and cut in neat slices. Noisette also means flavoured with hazelnuts, or butter cooked to a nut brown colour.

normande: a cooking style for fish, with a garnish of prawns (shrimp), mussels and mushrooms in a white wine cream sauce; for poultry and meat, a sauce with cream, Calvados and apple.

olive oil: various grades of oil extract from olives. Extra virgin olive oil has a full, fruity flavour and the lowest acidity. Virgin olive oil is slightly higher in acidity and lighter in flavour. Pure olive oil is a processed blend of olive oils and has the highest acidity and lightest taste.

panade: a mixture for binding stuffings and dumplings, notably quenelles, often of choux pastry or simply breadcrumbs. A panade may also be made of frangipane, pureed potatoes or rice.

papillote: to cook food in oiled or buttered greasepoof paper or aluminium foil. Also a decorative frill to cover bone ends of chops and poultry drumsticks.

parboil: to boil or simmer until part cooked (i.e. cooked further than when blanching).

pare: to cut away outside covering.

pate: a paste of meat or seafood used as a spread for toast or crackers.

paupiette: a thin slice of meat, poultry or fish spread with a savoury stuffing and rolled. In the United States this is also called "bird" and in Britain an "olive".

peel: to strip away outside covering.

plump: to soak in liquid or moisten thoroughly until full and round.

poach: to simmer gently in enough hot liquid to cover, using care to retain shape of food.

polyunsaturated fat: one of the three types of fats found in food. These exist in large quantities in such vegetable oils as safflower, sunflower, corn and soya bean. These fats lower the level of cholesterol in the blood.

puree: a smooth paste, usually of vegetables or fruits, made by putting foods through a sieve, food mill or liquefying in a blender or food processor.

ragout: traditionally a well-seasoned, rich stew containing meat, vegetables and wine. Nowadays, a term applied to any stewed mixture.

ramekins: small oval or round individual baking dishes.

reconstitute: to put moisture back into dehydrated foods by soaking in liquid.

reduce: to cook over a very high heat, uncovered, until the liquid is reduced by evaporation.

refresh: to cool hot food quickly, either under running water or by plunging it into iced water, to stop it cooking. Particularly for vegetables and occasionally for shellfish.

rice vinegar: mild, fragrant vinegar that is less sweet than cider vinegar and not as harsh as distilled malt vinegar. Japanese rice vinegar is milder than the Chinese variety.

roulade: a piece of meat, usually pork or veal, that is spread with stuffing, rolled and often braised or poached. A roulade may also be a sweet or savoury mixture that is baked in a Swiss roll tin or paper case, filled with a contrasting filling, and rolled.

rubbing-in: a method of incorporating fat into flour, by use of fingertips only. Also incorporates air into mixture.

safflower oil: the vegetable oil that contains the highest proportion of polyunsaturated fats.

salsa: a juice derived from the main ingredient being cooked or a sauce added to a dish to enhance its flavour. In Italy the term is often used for pasta sauces; in Mexico the name usually applies to uncooked sauces served as an accompaniment, especially to corn chips.

saturated fats: one of the three types of fats found in foods. These exist in large quantities in animal products, coconut and palm oils; they raise the level of cholesterol in the blood. As high cholesterol levels may cause heart disease, saturated fat consumption is recommended to be less than 15% of kilojoules provided by the daily diet.

sauté: to cook or brown in small amount of hot fat.

score: to mark food with cuts, notches of lines to prevent curling or to make food more attractive.

scald: to bring just to boiling point, usually for milk. Also to rinse with boiling water.

sear: to brown surface quickly over high heat in hot dish.

seasoned flour: flour with salt and pepper added.

sift: to shake a dry, powdered substance through a sieve or sifter to remove any lumps and give lightness.

simmer: to cook food gently in liquid that bubbles steadily just below boiling point so that the food cooks in even heat without breaking up.

singe: to quickly flame poultry to remove all traces of feathers after plucking.

skim: to remove a surface layer (often of impurities and scum) from a liquid with a metal spoon or small ladle.

slivered: sliced in long, thin pieces, usually refers to nuts, especially almonds.

soften: re gelatine - sprinkle over cold water and allow to gel (soften) then dissolve and liquefy.

souse: to cover food, particularly fish, in wine vinegar and spices and cook slowly; the food is cooled in the same liquid. Sousing gives food a pickled flavour.

steep: to soak in warm or cold liquid in order to soften food and draw out strong flavours or impurities.

stir-fry: to cook thin slices of meat and vegetable over a high heat in a small amount of oil, stirring constantly to even cooking in a short time. Traditionally cooked in a wok, however a heavy based frying pan may be used.

stock: a liquid containing flavours, extracts and nutrients of bones, meat, fish or vegetables.

stud: to adorn with; for example, baked ham studded with whole cloves.

sugo: an Italian sauce made from the liquid or juice extracted from fruit or meat during cooking.

sweat: to cook sliced or chopped food, usually vegetables, in a little fat and no liquid over very low heat. Foil is pressed on top so that the food steams in its own juices, usually before being added to other dishes.

timbale: a creamy mixture of vegetables or meat baked in a mould. French for "kettledrum"; also denotes a drum-shaped baking dish.

thicken: to make a thin, smooth paste by mixing together arrowroot, cornflour or flour with an equal amount of cold water; stir into hot liquid, cook, stirring until thickened.

toss: to gently mix ingredients with two forks or fork spoon.

total fat: the individual daily intake of all three fats previously described in this glossary. Nutritionists recommend that fats provide no more than 35% of the energy in the diet.

vine leaves: tender, lightly flavoured leaves of the grapevine, used in ethnic cuisine as wrappers for savoury mixtures. As the leaves are usually packed in brine, they should be well rinsed before use.

whip: to beat rapidly, incorporate air and produce expansion.

zest: thin outer layer of citrus fruits containing the aromatic citrus oil. It is usually thinly pared with a vegetable peeler, or grated with a zester or grater to separate it from the bitter white pith underneath.

INDEX

INDEX